# The
# MindBody
# ToolKit

## 10 Tools to Instantly Increase Your Energy, Enhance Productivity and Even Reverse Disease

### By
### Kim D'Eramo, D.O.

DrKimD.com

**#1 Amazon Best Seller**

# Disclaimer

Regarding Expectations of Results – Dr. Kim D'Eramo and the publisher accept no liability for the use or misuse of the information contained in this book. There is no possibility of substantiating any claimed results made or supplying any objective evidence, whether financial, business related, spiritual or otherwise. Dr. Kim D'Eramo and the publisher strongly advise that you seek professional advice as appropriate before making any health decision. It can be assumed that no results are to be expected as a result of one's purchase of this book. Dr. Kim D'Eramo and the publisher do not and cannot make any representations, promises or guarantees of the effectiveness of this book. That being said, Dr. Kim D'Eramo and her associates, partners and affiliates firmly believe in the effectiveness of the methods put forth in this book.

Published by Global Medical Innovations, LLC.
PO Box 957, Durango, CO 81302 USA

Cover Image: © Mike 301 | Dreamstime.com – Illustration of Vitruvian Man Photo

*Our true security and sense of worthiness comes not from our job, our accomplishments, our degrees or even our contribution to others.*

*True security is unwavering and stems from our own sense of self-acceptance and self-love. This heals the body and restores peace.*

*It is created within and is available to us all. Open with courage to receive this, and BE FULLY ALIVE. This will change the world.*

# Table of Contents

# Introduction

Have you been feeling burned out? Like life is a treadmill of continuous activity? Wouldn't it be nice if your body could just recharge instead of going, going, going?

We're all working too hard trying to make our lives work. We've been living in a society that trains us to focus outside ourselves for the answers and to expend our energy creating things externally. It's a results-focused mindset that neglects inner power. This is a world that applauds us not for the kind of person we become but for the achievements and accolades we collect. Even those of us without a medical diagnosis feel dried up and live in struggle on some level. As we've come through the last several decades, our health has suffered terribly from this imbalance.

Doctors have been taught to treat illness and reverse disease, and conventional medicine is excellent at preventing death and prolonging life. However, for a majority of patients, much is lacking in the current medical model. There are many modalities available today that add to our energy, vitality, performance, and wellbeing, which have been completely overlooked by our conventional system. The time has come for us to expand beyond pharmaceuticals and surgery to serve our patients in living, not just prevent them from dying.

So many patients have come to me in the emergency room struggling with pain, depression, or some form of chronic illness. There are a vast amount of medications I have used to treat these symptoms, but, for the majority of these patients, the source of their illness was not addressed.

Many patients want more than conventional medicine currently offers. These patients desire more than just living longer or continuing medication with harmful side effects. They want to feel vibrance and vitality, passion and exuberance coursing through their body. They want to perform at their peak potential, express their greatest gifts, and feel inspired throughout their day. They want to consistently experience their highest level of inspiration and aliveness in their relationships, career and outer life.

This level of aliveness is more than just possible, it is how our lives are meant to be. I have been studying and researching this for decades and am here as a physician to uncover how we can consistently attain these results.

While conventional medicine has many brilliant technologies, it has not really offered anything to help patients thrive. Medications can reverse symptoms, but they have limited value in connecting us with our Life Force, the source of healing within. When patients seeking to thrive look to their physicians, the doctor is often at a loss to offer something that can create this kind of impact, and may even tell the patient that it is not possible for them to feel this way.

*It isn't that doctors don't care deeply about their patients. In fact, most of them do! It's just that many of them have not been taught about the modalities that are available to create this possibility.*

As an osteopathic physician, I was taught to understand and appreciate that the source of healing lies within us. I would educate my patients about this, and treat them osteopathically to open them to this source and remove any barriers to receiving it. My results were sometimes limited, however. There were patients who would get better for a time, only to return with the same problems again and again:

depression, pain, and illness. I realized that although they would feel better physically, once they returned to their toxic relationships, toxic job situations and toxic ways of thinking, their physical vigor would eventually diminish. The ways they engaged in life limited their ability to really thrive.

If I wanted to assist my patients in making real changes in their health, I needed to assist them in making real changes in their life. *I needed to help them change the way they think.*

This desire revolutionized the approach I took in my career. I created an intensive course designed to educate patients about how to consistently access the vitality that is available to us all. In this course, I taught that it is our thoughts and beliefs that either open us to the Life Force or limit our experience of it. Even the way we respond to medication and medical procedures is dependent upon our thoughts and beliefs. Our ability to experience this Life Force within creates healthy, vibrant cells, healthy, vibrant emotions, and a healthy vibrant life – or the lack thereof.

This book will give you an introduction to connecting with your Life Force and provide specific tools that will help you experience it in ever-increasing amounts. This means more energy and productivity, more inspired ideas and creativity, more ease, and a greater sense of fulfillment and wellbeing.

It is essential that you connect this way if you are to attain your life purpose, live to your full potential, and do what you came here to do. My intention is that we each individually embrace this power within ourselves and create a world filled with vitality, inspiration, prosperity, and peace.

I have created several resources that will help you on your own journey to vibrant health and prosperity. You can download yours absolutely free at:

## DrKimD.com/Resources

# The Premise of This Book

When I was a child, my siblings and I would play a game where one of us would have to find something hidden. If I walked toward the item, they would say, *"You're getting hot!"* If I walked in the wrong direction, they would say, *"Cold!"* The closer I got to the item, the more they would yell: *"HOT! Smoking! Steaming!"* or *"You're on fire!"* to indicate that I was very, very close. When I was very close and turned away even slightly, they would indicate that I was cold or even freezing. The closer I got, the more precise my indicator would be.

As a living, breathing human being, your body is constantly communicating to you whether you are hot or cold too. What you are moving toward or away from is your ideal state. This ideal state is the state of "Thriving."

Thriving is living in full vitality when your body heals itself and you are supported in a fulfilled, enriching life. You express your natural gifts, strengths and talents and experience your value in the world. There is harmony and purpose in your life, your relationships and your work. This is your Truth.

When you have thoughts that are counter to your Truth, your body and your life give you signals that you are cold. You don't feel well, you have low energy, things are difficult for you, and nothing goes your way. When you have thoughts that are in sync with your Truth, your body feels good. You have increased energy and vitality. Life around you also responds and things seem to work themselves out for you effortlessly.

As a physician, I am intimately familiar with the signals and communication pathways in the body. I understand the physiology behind our internal states. Throughout this book, I explain this physiology for you, so that you understand what is happening within your body, how nature designed you, and how your internal guidance system works. I offer the ten best lessons or tools that I use (and that I've not taught to countless patients and course participants to use) to access their life force and live in full vitality. I share some of my favorite quotes and answer the most common questions that come up in my courses regarding each tool. Each chapter ends with a MindBody Prescription, an exercise for you to use at any time during your day to integrate this tool into your life. Following this, I've given you an affirmation or meditation to complete the process.

These processes, when applied several times throughout the day, have been shown to create actual changes in your brain structure. These tools allow your brain to lay down new neurologic connections to carry this new type of information. This is powerful! That means even if you've been depressed for years, you can create a new baseline for how you feel every day by practicing what I've laid out here.

I recommend setting the alarm in your phone to remind you to practice a particular tool. Use the affirmation in the alarm title, so you put your phone to work to give you a chemical lift multiple times during the day. When the alarm goes off, do the "MindBody Prescription" and spend a minute focusing your attention integrating that tool into your MindBody system. Think of it as mental exercise…so you need less physical exercise!

## The Chemistry of A Thriving Body

What does it mean to truly thrive? Thriving is the experience of your highest vision of vitality and aliveness in all areas of life. It's that feeling of being turned on and fully alive. Thriving is that state of completion and fulfillment for which we are all longing. It is your natural state and it is your birthright.

You do not need to be someone special or accomplish something significant to experience this level of vitality. It happens when you are aligned with your life's purpose and highest level of self-expression. You thrive when you live as who you authentically are. You thrive when you function at peak potential and deliver value to others. You can connect with this state at any time from whatever state you are in. You don't need to wait. This state of full aliveness and vitality is available to you right now!

How you think about yourself and your life has a lot to do with whether you experience life in health and fulfillment or you don't. Your mind is actually in charge of all of your experiences.

*Every thought you have is a chemical reaction in your body.*

These reactions have either positive or negative effects. Your thoughts affect every cell in your body and also have an effect on how you feel. Your entire internal state actually begins with your thoughts. It is your internal state that drives all of your actions and behaviors and dictates every single thing you do.

When you have "negative" thoughts, thoughts that go against your natural state and against your Truth, you generate chemicals that are damaging to your cells. Any thoughts that cause anxiety, fear, anger, or even just frustration and irritability generate these "negative chemicals." These stressful thoughts ignite the fight-or-flight response in the body. Cortisol, epinephrine and norepinephrine, and the inflammatory cascade kick in and have an effect on all of your cells.

These stress chemicals assist you in the short term, fueling the muscles, focusing the brain, increasing blood pressure and heart rate and making the heart pump more powerfully. The problem occurs when these hormones and stress chemicals are around for extended periods of time.

Over time, these effects are harmful and cause

cells to break down. The body is not designed to withstand chronic, ongoing exposure to these biochemicals. However, for people living in intense states of anxiety and tension, these hormones stick around for much longer than intended and wreak havoc on the body. The heart is overworked, the blood vessels become damaged, and organ function is impaired. We see the effects of this throughout our culture; chronic illnesses like heart disease, diabetes, and cancer are now rampant.

During this stress state, these biochemicals shunt blood away from the brain and digestive system to fuel the working muscles. Therefore, in this state you do not properly break down and absorb nutrients the way you need to. Since these chemicals inhibit insulin, the body needs to secrete more insulin to get the blood sugar down. This high insulin state promotes fat storage, and we are not able to break down fats for energy so weight gain occurs.

For short-term periods of stress or intensity, it is useful for our brain to be focused on one thing and think of nothing other than the task at hand; however, in this stress state we are unable to see the bigger picture. With chronic stress, the brain cannot process large amounts of information, and does not have the insight to create solutions, even simple ones that are right in front of our faces.

Does this help you understand why so many people seem to be "out of their minds?" We often make irrational choices that work against the things we most want- eating foods that make us ill, working hard to get nowhere, and creating chaos in our relationships…simply because our brain is in the stress state and cannot compute.

Also during this stress state, the vessels that feed the organs constrict to shunt the blood to the working muscles. This deprives the organs and tissues of oxygen and nutrients. Cells deteriorate and build up toxic waste products. This negative chemical state even affects your DNA and turns "on" the genes for diseases like diabetes, heart disease and cancer.

*Limiting, "negative" thoughts destroy you at the level of your cells and your DNA.*

When you have "positive" thoughts, thoughts that are in sync with your natural vitality, this generates "positive biochemistry" that is nurturing to your cells.

Endorphins and oxytocin make you feel good. Antioxidants repair damage in your DNA and reverse illness and ageing. The immune system is strengthened and you are resistant to pathogens like bacteria and viruses. Your serotonin and other hormones balance out and create harmony.

You feel good because your brain works as it is meant to, processing the big picture and easily processing information to come up with creative solutions to make your life work. Even your DNA expression is affected so that healthy genes that strengthen your system and protect against illness are turned on and the genes for disease are turned off.

*Life-giving, "positive" thoughts protect and strengthen you at the level of your cells and DNA!*

## Your Many Minds

Most people think of the mind being centered in the brain; and for decades, this was the scientific and medical understanding. The brain was thought to govern activity for all the areas of the body, and be the sole producer of neurotransmitters, the hormones that deliver information to the entire nervous system. Extensive research by Harvard's Benson-Henry Institute for Mind Body Medicine has now demonstrated that this is not true.

There are networks of nerve cells or "thinking cells," located all over the body, and distributed throughout the various organs: heart, lungs, kidneys, liver, thyroid, etc. Your mind and your body are fully integrated and cannot be separated. As soon as you have a thought, the message is instantaneously transmitted throughout every cell in your body. There isn't a single cell that does not register the impact of that thought, no matter how short lived.

In the medical textbooks, we're taught that the brain cells operate separately from the other systems of the body. Mind and body are seen as distinct, so it's easy to understand how we've failed to deal with them together when it comes to medical treatment. However, in your actual system, your mind and body are one.

A large proportion of these neural networks are located in the area around the heart. These nerve networks around the heart respond to neurotransmitters (brain chemicals) in the same way the brain does. Interestingly, the nerves in the area of the heart send large amounts information and signals to the brain that control brain activity. In fact, there is more information from the heart going to the brain to control and modulate brain function than from the brain to control the heart.

*The research has shown that the heart and emotional state play a far more significant role in controlling brain function and organ activity than previously thought.*

In fact, studies by The Center of Heart Math have found that the nerve activity around the level of the heart can be measured to have impact throughout the body and even beyond the body. This electromagnetic energy of the heart can be detected at distances of *up to eight to ten feet away from the body.*

The cellular activity in the nerve cells around

the heart creates a field of electromagnetic energy that changes depending on the emotional state of the person. This activity is considered either "concordant" or "discordant." The "concordant" activity harmonizes organ function: evening out the heart rate, normalizing blood pressure, and instilling smooth respiratory function. The "discordant" activity causes erratic variability in the heart rate, irregularity in the breathing, and abnormal shifts in the blood pressure.

The "concordant" activity is detected in the area around the heart when a person is experiencing harmonic emotions, such as love, joy, peace and appreciation. "Discordant" activity is detected from the area around the heart when a person is experiencing disharmonic emotional states like anger, fear, frustration or impatience. The more negative the emotional state, the more erratic and disharmonic is the physiologic activity detected in the vital signs. Therefore, your *emotional state* is directly linked to the quality of physiologic activity in your body.

# Your Emotions: The Key to Your Every Thought

There are many neurologic transmissions and thoughts traveling through the mind at any given time. It would be impossible to keep track of them all. The thoughts you are aware of are only the tip of the iceberg, since most of your thoughts are unconscious. However, you *do* have the ability to become aware of what is going on at any time. Your emotions are the key to this awareness.

*Your emotional state reflects the sum total of all the thoughts you are having at any given time.*

You can become aware of your emotions by connecting to how you feel. This takes practice. For decades society has trained us to use our left brain in processing information, rationalizing, and figuring things out. We have been trained to ignore our feelings, because they were thought to be irrelevant. However, your emotions have immense value! They give you immediate insight as to whether the way you are thinking is generating a positive or a negative response in your body. When your thinking is generating a negative response (creating cellular damage), you have lower emotions: anger, anxiety, fear. When your thinking generates a positive response (enhancing cellular health), you feel higher emotions: joy, love, inspiration or appreciation. It is through accessing your emotions that you become aware of the impact of the thoughts and beliefs you are holding, and any choice you may be considering.

If you were to rely on left-brained, rational thinking alone in making choices, do you have any idea how much information you would need to process before you could make an informed decision? Let's say you are deciding on what college is best for your child. You think about the location, the quality of education, the safety, the price of tuition, and many other important factors. Even if you could solidly nail down which school had the best mix of all of these factors, you still could not know which would provide your child the best mix of friends, social support, inspirational experiences, and opportunities for his or her ideal career and life.

How would you best make the choice then? You would gather all of the important information....and you would then base your decision on *how you feel.*

Even if you think you are the most rational person you know, and you think everything through before making a choice, I would tell you that your emotions are still running the show. When you walk into a room, your emotions determine where you choose to sit. Someone smells funny to you or someone has looks that make you feel uncomfortable. This type of awareness is happening *way* below the level of your conscious mind – you think you just liked the seat in the middle.

Let's say you want to get fit and lose weight. You have all the best intentions to get to the gym but you're tired, or hungry or someone calls you on the phone, so you decide not to go. You think you chose not to go to the gym because it made more sense to take that call or eat dinner, but the reason you didn't go is because your emotional state prevented you from going. *Period.*

It is your emotions that are inspiring you or dragging you down. When you are emotionally aligned with a certain outcome, your emotions trigger reminders and motivation to bring that outcome about. You remember that it's time for an appointment or time to eat. So you arrive at your destination on time, or you eat a meal. It is your emotional state that drives your every action or behavior.

You can use the awareness of your emotional state to make shifts in your thinking (and therefore your life.) When you are in a negative emotional state, your choices and decisions will create results that reflect that negative state back to you. This happens automatically, unless you become aware and shift your emotional state.

*Becoming aware of your internal state gives you a choice: you can react or you can shift your state.*

You can be reactive and function on autopilot…or you can choose to shift your emotional state *first*, before acting, speaking, or doing anything. It is that simple. It becomes that easy.

The next section of the book contains 10 MindBody Tools to use in shifting your emotional state in any given moment. The more you practice them, the more ingrained they become until this way of being is your autopilot and you effortlessly create a life that reflects what you want. Even with initial use, however, you will begin to see major shifts in the reality you are experiencing.

It is my intention that you keep an open mind in allowing your personal transformation, being willing to persist in using your mind as the brilliant and powerful creative tool that it really is.

I invite your questions and comments on the Facebook page created especially for this work:

http://bit.ly/MindBodyCommunity

Join now and share: *Why are you reading this book and what benefit are you ready to receive as a result of this work?* I will support you!

# MindBody Tool #1: Change Your Thoughts

*"Let a man radically alter his thoughts, and he will be astonished at the rapid transformation it will effect in the material conditions of his life."*
*— James Allen*

## Fighting An Uphill Battle

Are you working against yourself? If you are harboring negative thoughts or beliefs while doing things to get ahead and succeed in life, then the answer is a resounding "YES!" So powerful are your thoughts that they can negate the benefits of even the best fitness routines and the healthiest of diets.

I can't count the number of patients I have seen who deeply want to be healthy and feel great, but who have not even begun to get to the root cause of why they are feeling depressed, carrying excess weight, or experiencing illness. Many toil away at the gym, take all kinds of supplements, do a cleanse, visit the doctor or another kind of practitioner...all to no avail. If they do see results, they are hard-won and fleeting. When they tire out the weight comes back, they have a pain flare up, or they go back to being anxious and depressed.

This happens because the root cause of imbalance and disease begins in your thoughts and beliefs. It won't matter what you do on the outside if your beliefs and thoughts are not aligned with what you are trying to achieve. It is your thoughts that create your internal conditions and your chemistry. It is your thoughts that create your emotional state, which drives all of your actions and behaviors. If you want a change in your life, *change your thoughts*. When you change your mind you change your health; you change your life.

## Chemical Warfare

When you are in the stress state, the "fight-or-flight nervous system" (called the *sympathetic nervous system*) turns on, and you immediately inhibit health. The stress hormones: cortisol, epinephrine, and norepinephrine, weaken the immune system, speed up the ageing process, increase blood pressure and heart rate, and cause "inflammation."

*The inflammatory stress state is a chemical war against our own cells.*

This inflammation is the chemical process that underlies every major chronic illness most Americans are currently dying from: Heart Disease, Type 2 Diabetes, Stroke, Obesity, and others. It is also the chemistry behind autoimmune illnesses and pain syndromes like Arthritis, Lupus, Chronic Fatigue, Crohn's Disease, Ulcerative Colitis, Fibromyalgia…and many more chronic illnesses experienced by millions today.

## The Relaxation Response

When you enter a positive state, the opposite occurs. The *parasympathetic nervous system* re-establishes balance, and health is restored. This is known as the *"Relaxation Response."* The Relaxation Response is the term coined by Herbert Benson, M.D. from Harvard Medical School, who has studied the healing effects of the relaxation response extensively and documented this in numerous studies over the past 40 years.

*The relaxation response has been definitively shown to reverse virtually every disease state known to man.*

Yes, genetics plays a role. Yes, what you eat affects your health. Yes, exercise does make you feel great. But the impact of these is minor compared to the power of the millions of thoughts you are having in every moment. Even a person with a terrible genetic predisposition can exhibit perfect health when his thoughts are aligned with what makes him thrive.

## Why Affirmations Don't Work

How can you change your thoughts if you don't even know what most of them are? Since most of your thoughts are unconscious, you could hold the conscious thought: *"I'm a great success"* and still feel like a total loser because of the quality of your unconscious thoughts. It seems like you're thinking a positive thought….but nothing's really changing. That's because that one thought is really just a drop in the bucket of the vast amount of thoughts coursing through your mind. You can't possibly be aware of them all.

That is where accessing your emotions comes in. You *can* become aware of your emotional state in any given moment. You immediately override and shift all of your negative thoughts by getting yourself into a higher emotional state.

*To change your thoughts, access your emotions.*

How would it feel to be living your ideal life? How would you feel if you were a massive success with plenty of money, a beautiful lover and a healthy, fit body? Beyond thinking about it… Can you *feel* the effect of that thought?

When you can get into that *feeling* and embrace it, letting it wash over you and bathe your cells, you actually make it infinitely more likely that that you will experience that outcome. *You basically draw the experience to you.*

How does this work?

## How Feeling Your Body Saves Your Cells

Your emotions are chemicals too. So when you change your emotional state (by feeling this outcome you want), you change your chemistry and change the cellular messages going on inside your body. You initiate the positive chemical state of the relaxation response when you *feel* your desired outcome.

Endorphins and oxytocin (feel-good hormones) increase, hormonal balance occurs, oxidation and toxicity decrease, and you feel better. When you are in the state of feeling your desired outcome, the fight-or-flight response of the sympathetic nervous system gets turned off. Cortisol and stress hormones decrease and your body restores normal function. Inflammation decreases so your body is no longer reactive and irritated. The parasympathetic nervous system (that's the relaxation response that makes you healthy) kicks in and allows physiologic balance. You absorb nutrients, excrete waste, and oxygenate your organs and tissues. Basically, your body functions in the health that it's meant to be in.

When you get into the emotional state that matches your desired outcome, you begin to establish better health, *instantaneously,* and you behave in ways that are consistent with thriving because you feel great.

Also, since positive emotions harmonize the mind cells at the level of the heart, your physiology is balanced and brain function improves. Have you ever been in a stressful experience and not been able to find the right words, stumbling and blundering…and then later, when the situation is long over, the witty words that would have brought perfect resolution come to mind? That's because you are no longer in the stress state.

# What the Relaxation Response Does for Performance

When you are in the "relaxation state," the right words come effortlessly, and you have insight in how to perfectly handle situations.

In this relaxation state, your proprioception (that's your balance and coordination) is enhanced, and you perform better at whatever you are doing. If you're a tennis player and you want to win, generating a positive emotional state by embracing positive thoughts will actually bring about enhanced performance and you're more likely to win!

If you are nervous about a meeting or a date, conjuring up winning thoughts and generating an emotional shift *first* will enhance your ability to be yourself and have the impact you want to have. You end up with wins at work or fun on a date.

This is why:

*When you think you are a success, you find that you are!*

...and vice versa. What you are thinking sets the stage for your outcome, even if you try to work against it. If you're really persistent and strong, you may be able to pull it off...but inevitably you will be overcome. It's your nature. You cannot fool your own cells.

## Why Your Thoughts Can Make You Unsuccessful

If your underlying thoughts are *"My body is disgusting,"* but you work hard to lose weight, you may at first see some results. Let's say you start working out, changing your eating and drinking more water. You lose some weight or feel more energized, but you haven't done anything to *change the way you think* about your body. Eventually you get fed up with vegetables, stop exercising, and start drinking soda again. Where do you think those soda cravings come from? Your own chemistry, which is impacted by your thoughts!

This is true not only in your relationship with your body, but also with everyone around you. That's why if you tell your children to calm down, but inside you're impatient and frustrated, they won't calm down. They are following your lead.

The reason you can't override your thoughts and internal state is because they get communicated in everything you do. Ninety-three percent of what you communicate is in your body language, tone, volume, and pace, not in your content. These things cannot be faked. These are subconscious communications. They impact on everything around you.

Think of a nervous person, filled with fear and anxiety and having thoughts like: *"I'm a loser and everyone knows it."* How would his voice sound if he were to say: *"Respect me. I'm worth listening to!"* Would you listen to this person and follow?

Now think of that same person holding thoughts of *power*. He feels certain and confidant, and says: *"I am a massive success and can do anything I choose."* He has fully embodied this empowered emotional state. Would you rely on this person? Would you follow?

When you think winning thoughts and generate a matching emotional state, it comes across in your communication and you have impact and power. This affects your work and all of your relationships. That's why when you feel like you're worthless, others treat you as such. They can't not!

*Others    are    receiving    your    unconscious*

*communication, and it's more powerful than your words.*

Your impact and affect on others is directly related to your internal state. Everyone knows what is going on inside you on a subconscious level, and they will respond and treat you accordingly, even if they have no idea why.

Your life will always reflect your thoughts about yourself. Choose thriving thoughts, and you create a thriving life. Feel the emotions of your desired outcome, and you generate thoughts and brain activity that match it.

# MindBody Prescription

Consider these empowering thoughts and tune into the way they make you feel:
- *"I am worthy of love and belonging."*
- *"I am brilliant and valuable."*
- *"I am healthy and filled with vitality."*

Hold that feeling in your body for several breaths and receive it. Breathe this way until you feel an emotional shift inside.

# Question:
***Isn't this unrealistic? How can I think these positive thoughts when I know they are not true?***

There is a difference between your truth and the *Real* Truth. Your current experience is true and is real for you. It isn't necessarily the Real Truth, however. It's just your interpretation of reality. The Real Truth is that life responds to your beliefs, and you will always see evidence to support what you currently think. It takes willingness to consider a new possibility and to begin to embrace a different experience before you see evidence of that new belief. You are right that your experience is really happening and the limitations you have are really true for you. You can also let that go and embrace a new truth and choose to live it. You can be right or you can be happy. You choose.

Let the new thoughts in, even if they are not apparent in your reality. Begin to base your thoughts and beliefs not on what you are currently experiencing, but on what you would like to be true. Choose thoughts that make you feel how you would like to feel.

Question your beliefs. Find your most negative belief and ask: *"Can I know for sure that this is actually true? Have I had any experiences that this idea is not true?"*

For example: *"I need to work hard to have money."* Do you know anyone who doesn't work hard and who has plenty of money? Do you know anyone who works very hard and still has no money?

Begin to question your conclusions and create space for new ideas and beliefs.

## Affirmation
*"I stay in a state of ease and grace, and life reflects this back to me."*
<u>DrKimD.com/Resources</u>

# MindBody Tool #2: Remember Your ABC's – "Awaken, Breathe, Choose"

*"Be still and know that I am God."*
*— Psalm 46:10*

How often have you started your day and known that it was or was not going to be a "good" day? How often have you felt subject to external circumstances that seemed to dictate whether your day would or would not go well?

Does it feel sometimes like your entire life is subject to random chance dictating whether or not things will turn out the way you want them to?

It's time to wake up!

*Your experience of life is entirely within your own control, and you have the ability to make your life what you want it to be.*

You just haven't learned where the controls are. Maybe you never realized that you are actually the one in control. No wonder life has not turned out the way you want it to.

Forgive yourself for what you have created thus far, let go of the past, and get in the driver's seat. In this chapter I'm going to show you how to use some of the controls.

*Your thoughts affect every cell in your body.*

They generate the chemical state that sets the stage for everything that happens in your body, and they set up your emotional state. Your thoughts also create. On a quantum level, reality is made of all the same stuff, and this stuff is energy. Your thoughts have an energetic impact on everything around you and even things remote.

Most of your thoughts are unconscious; they're pre-programmed and run on autopilot creating the same things over and over again. You don't need to understand biochemistry or physics to put the particles of matter together and create; your energetic system is creating your life for you.

The experience of reality you are currently creating will match the emotional state you are in now. So get a handle on where you are right now. From there, all you need to do is bring yourself to a better emotional state, which develops better-feeling thoughts. Since your thoughts create your life, you develop a better experience of life!

How do you raise your emotional state? I've come up with a simple method you can use in any given moment.

I call it the "Instant Elevation Technique."

# The Instant Elevation Technique: A, B, C

## A. Awaken

Become aware of how you are feeling right now. Do this on a scale of 0–10, ten being the best. Rate your emotional level and acknowledge it.

Just your *awareness* of your internal state actually shifts your chemistry immediately. This shift occurs because it changes the thoughts you are having and the quality of your attention. You shift from having unconscious thoughts, which are usually negative and limiting, to being consciously aware and focusing on your internal state.

Typically you only awaken to become aware of your internal state when you are struggling, hurting, or otherwise experiencing something that you do not want. The pain becomes so severe it wakes you up. That's a good thing…although it may not feel so great. Sometimes the pain and discomfort may get so bad, you find yourself on your knees asking for a way out. It doesn't matter how bad you feel, what matters is that you awaken. Become aware of how you feel.

Most people live in an unawakened state. In this state, the subconscious programming runs the show for your life. The subconscious is your default mode, and studies show that more than 70% of our unconscious thoughts are negative. Until you align your mind with the beliefs you want, life will not be fulfilling.

You can live in default mode, only becoming aware at the points of suffering, or you can choose to practice consciously awakening at any time. Do this simply by focusing on your internal state. This happens in the present moment. Set your alarm to remind you.

Emotions are meant to be felt. E-motion is energy-in-motion, and the energy in your body must move for you to be fully alive and healthy. When you become aware, you tune into what's going on inside your body now. You feel what's happening in there...and then you can move it! (That's next.)

The fastest way I've found to become awaken is by feeling your body. You just bring your attention into your physical body and focus on how it feels. Your body *only* lives in the "Now" so this practice immediately gets your mind out of past or future focus. Most of us spend most of our time not present, not in our body, not in the Now. Our attention is focused on the past, and what we did or didn't do, what someone did or didn't do to us, what we regret, or what we are angry about. These are all past.

We can also spend time in the future, thinking about what we need to do, what we hope happens, or what we fear will happen. Connecting in your body and becoming aware of your internal state is the remedy for this!

Your internal state is never something in the past or something in the future. It can only exist Now!

*Becoming aware of your body anchors you in the Now.*

This moment, right Now, is where everything REAL is happening. Nothing unreal (past, future, hypothetical) exists in your body right now. Turn off your past angers, resentments, regrets and sorrows.

Turn off your future worries, anxieties, fears and concerns. Get into your body *Now*... and just feel what IS.

## B. Breathe

Take three deep, present, mindful breaths.

The breath actually has the ability to transform your chemical and energetic state *immediately*. When you slow your breath down and breathe into your belly instead of your chest, you change from the fight-or-flight breathing to the relaxation breathing.

Relax your shoulders away from your ears and let your spine lengthen up straight. Slowly let the breath come in as your belly balloons out. Then relax and let the air come out as your belly sinks back in. Take three to ten breaths like this now…and anytime you feel stressed or have any emotion that you would like to shift.

This way of breathing is how your body processes and moves energy.

Remember, we are energetic beings. We're made of energy. Our bodies' cells are made of molecules, which are made of atoms, which are made of subatomic particles, which are entirely comprised of just plain energy waves. When we look closely with the most powerful microscope, we see that the smallest particles are not particulate at all, they're just energy waves!

*Your body is made of energy waves.*

Moving and circulating energy is completely essential to being a fully alive, vibrant human being. You must allow this type of relaxed breathing in order for your body to properly release old emotional energy and make space to process and receive new energy. Think of this breathing system like the digestive system for your emotional body.

During fight-or-flight, we aren't processing emotions. Would you really want to be feeling sad over your lover leaving you while you're trying to outrun a tiger? No. You do that later, when you've found a safe haven to rest. The problem is, most of us never get to that resting place. We keep going and going, so the emotions, which are meant to grow us and expand our ability to feel exhilarated and alive, stay stuck in the body for "later." However, when energy gets stuck in our bodies, we become tired, depressed, anxious, overweight, and diseased.

This type of breathing also affects us chemically. It generates the positive chemical state. It turns off the sympathetic nervous system, (stress response, cortisol, epinephrine, inflammation, limited ability to process new information) and turns on the parasympathetic nervous system (hormonal balance, oxytocin, endorphins, restoration of energy).

Breathing this way shifts the nerve activity in the brain and changes the information that the brain registers. Areas of the brain that store positive thoughts are activated, and positive thoughts are triggered. This type of breathing gives you an expanded perspective and the ability to process new information, and makes you feel better immediately.

*Breathing changes your brain and chemistry.*

Your sympathetic nervous system cells are located inside the back of the ribcage where the ribs meet your spine. When you breathe into the ribcage instead of the belly, these nerve cells get activated. That's why even if you try to calm down and "think positive" you still feel anxious! When chest breathing (fight or flight breathing) is your default mode, you will feel anxious even when everything around you is just fine. The message sent to your nervous system is: "Gear up! It's time to fight or flee!"

The diaphragm muscle is located at the junction between the ribcage and belly. When you use "diaphragmatic breathing," as I've described above, your diaphragm muscle comes down and flattens out, allowing the ribcage to expand outward instead of upward. The diaphragm, which is the "primary muscle of respiration" does all the work so the "secondary muscles of respiration" in your chest, back and neck can relax. Ahhhh...

It's a subtle shift, but makes all the difference to your nervous system. You will feel it in just a few breaths!

# C.  Choose

Now that you've relaxed your nervous system, neck and back muscles and turned off the fight-or-flight brain patterns, you can make conscious choices that get you what you really want!

You've created an expanded and aware state after slowing things down with the breath, so you are able to choose your actions rationally. When you are in this state, things are so much easier than they seem when we are stressed! You have allowed your hormones to balance, slowed down your brain wave activity from the frenetic pace of stress, and improved your emotional state. Everything will appear different in this new state. Now you can make choices that really serve you.

The simplest way to apply "C" is simply by making a conscious choice to expand. You acknowledge that you are feeling contracted (your system has been shut down and tight) and you would like to feel expanded (free, easy and flowing).

*Simply stating: "I choose to feel better" is enough.*

A more specific way to apply "C" is to make the specific choices that you know will bring about a better result. If you're in the middle of a conversation, you may choose to be still and silent instead of defending yourself or insulting the other person. (This subtle shift in choice can save a marriage.) You may realize that you don't really need that piece of chocolate cake or fried chicken and instead make another food choice. There are a myriad of choices available to you at any moment, and now you are in a state where you're free to choose something different.

Typically, you already know everything you need to know about what to do to create the outcomes you want. You probably have an idea of some choices that are appropriate: exercise, eat vegetables, get plenty of sleep, be compassionate with others, treat yourself with kindness, etc. …So why don't you do them?

When you're in a stress state, you don't make these choices easily. You have food cravings and grab whatever's available. You criticize others and speak harshly. You feel sluggish and sit around instead of going for a walk. This happens because you are reacting to external situations. You're not proactive in your life; you're *reactive* when you live in the stress state.

You haven't been able to make the choices that make you thrive, because when things are coming at you so fast, you can't even see the options.

I had a patient who told me he'd spent tens of thousands of dollars on medical bills and treatment and was interested in participating in my program. He was eager to work with me, but was worried because he'd tried so many other things in the past that hadn't worked. "Dr.Kim, how come all the things I've learned to do to be healthy I just don't do? I know I'm supposed to get more sleep and eat better foods, and I've read so many books about this...but I haven't been able to change anything! What am I not getting?"

This man had learned plenty about how to take care of himself, stay youthful and live at ideal weight. That was not what was missing. What he needed was to repattern his hardwiring (which is exactly what my programs are about)! We're never tired, ill, or overweight for the reasons we think we are. This man had been trying to address the problem from the same mindset where it was created. No matter how hard he tried, he simply couldn't lose weight and generate real change.

The issue wasn't simply that he didn't eat right, or sleep enough, or exercise often. He was overweight and tired because his system was constantly in the stress state and he had no other choice.

When I taught him how to shift this state using the Instant Elevation Technique, he immediately signed up for my program...and later told me it was one of the best decisions he'd ever made. He was now easily following all the advice he'd spent decades learning, and has successfully lost the weight.

For most of us, these choices are simply not available. Either we're too busy to eat right, too tired to exercise, and too irritable to treat others kindly. We end up creating the problems we're working so hard to fix!

When you wake up and shift your internal state by using your breath to slow things down, you feel better and you make better choices. These choices impact every level of your experience, and are the habits for your thriving life.

## MindBody Prescription

Allow your abdomen to relax and balloon out as you take in slow, deep, breaths and allow whatever is going on to just be.

Watch your internal state by focusing your attention on how this feels. Allow it to just *be* without following the impulse to do anything about it.

Hold that awareness in your body for several breaths and receive whatever comes in. Breathe this way until you feel an emotional shift inside.

## Question:
***"How can I stop when something really needs my attention? I have to react quickly or it will not be okay."***

No matter what you are doing, you must breathe. As an Emergency Medicine doctor, I have been in life or death situations many times. It may seem that I especially, need to keep a fast pace and stay in "fight or flight," however, even in a true emergency, this tool is an asset. Nowhere in my life has it been so apparent the importance of breathing and slowing things down.

When I'm stressed I can't think straight, it's impossible to recall the myriad of medications and algorithms I need to access. When I get present and breathe mindfully, my actions have the impact I want them to have.

Getting present using the Instant Elevation Tool gives allows me to do everything from quickly calculating the correct drug dosage to easily performing life-saving procedures. When you slow down and breathe this way, you can use your mind as the brilliant machine it really is.

Trust this tool and let it work for you. It changes everything and makes life magical.

## Meditation

Think of something that is causing you distress. Use the breathing above and let whatever is bothering you leave with the exhaled breath.

Just exhale it out. See this old energy leaving you. Bring in peace and love as you inhale. See your body fill up with light as you receive each breath.

Do this several times a day and any time you would like to feel free, joyful, secure, or clear-headed.

Kim D'Eramo, D.O.

# MindBody Tool #3: Focus on What You *DO* Want

*"Problems cannot be solved with the same mindset that created them."*
— *Albert Einstein*

Often when we're dealing with something we don't want, we try to figure it out and do something to make it better. When nothing changes, we try harder, then begin to feel powerless and worry that it won't get better. We may complain and gripe to a friend, wondering why this thing is happening to us. We think we just *have* to talk about it, focus on it, and figure it out. Then, we can do something about it and make a change. It seems "venting" is making us feel better, and so we keep airing out our problems. Sometimes our lives revolve around them!

It's typical to focus on what you don't want when we're dealing with a challenge, because things that are bothersome get our attention. As a doctor, this happens all the time. People come to me to address their problems and complaints. They focus on what's wrong. We focus on it together, then come up with ways to change it.

It feels like a natural way to go about things…but it's not the way the life force in your body works to heal you, and it's not how problems get resolved.

## Look Where You're Going!

I remember one time I was riding my bike down a hill toward a busy street. I was going fast and saw a huge pothole in front of me. The thought that went through my head was: *"Do NOT hit that pothole!"* The next thing that happened was me flipping over my handlebars.

My focus of attention was on the pothole, *not* on the areas around the pothole. In order to go around the pothole, that's where I need to be looking. I've heard the same thing from many other cyclists. You must focus on the area where you *do* want to go and put your attention there!

Doctors have been trained to focus on the symptoms and the disease, and patients are accustomed to think in terms of their problems. This happens not only in medicine, but in every area of life. We bring our attention onto the things we *don't* want in an effort to change them into the things we *do* want, without giving much attention to what that actually is!

Even when people talk about what they do want, it's framed in terms of what they do not want: *"I hope I don't get sick," "I don't want to go into debt." "I want to get out of this pain." "I don't want to date any more losers."*

It's time to retrain your brain.

## Retrain Your Brain

*What you focus on expands.* Whatever you put your mind on creates your internal state. When you focus your attention on what you *DO* want it feels good. Why? There are several reasons for this.

When you bring your attention to what you *do* want, you immediately begin to generate the positive chemicals that nourish your cells and create a higher emotional state. Oxytocin and endorphins block pain receptors and stimulate the receptors for pleasure, so you get relief from focusing on your pain or discontent. You literally generate internal morphine. It's been shown in studies that when patients are in higher emotional states like love and joy, their pain threshold is higher and they need less pain medication.

*Your cells are listening and responding to your every thought.*

When you focus your attention on what you *do* want, you feel better, and it becomes easier to see the positive side of things. This means it's easier to keep focusing on what you *do* want and to think of even more things that make you feel good.

A friend of mine, Gay Hendricks, relays this point perfectly. He was on a long bike ride and felt amazing. The day was beautiful, he was energized and fueled, and he looked forward to a wonderful ride. As he rode by a friend's home, many positive thoughts came to mind. He appreciated this friend who had been in his life for so many years, and lovingly thought of all they'd gone through together. He was proud of his friend for persisting in his quest for love and partnership and finding his now wife.

Later, on the way back from a grueling ride, hungry and fatigued, he rode by the same friend's home. This time he became aware of how irritated he was that this friend hadn't contacted him recently and it occurred to him that his friend has always been a bit selfish. He thought about the fact that this friend is now on his third marriage and resented him for being immature and unevolved.

Gay, being a person who has extensive practice with these types of MindBody tools, appreciated his mind for all it was reflecting, and let the thoughts go. He laughed and shook it off knowing the only thing he needed to do to fix any of this was to have a good meal and get some rest.

Your mind is constantly painting a picture of the world depending on the state you are in. In the positive chemical state, the mind is able to process information more easily and opens to new insights and creative solutions you previously could not see. Since the mind is able to see the big picture, you can see beyond the problem, making it easier to keep your focus on what you DO want.

Here is the most interesting part:

*Focusing on what you do want changes the hardwiring of your brain.*

## Neuroplasticity

The nerve cells in the brain connect to other nerve cells at junctions called synapses. These neural synapses are constructed in a certain pattern, or formation, so the same information gets transmitted over and over along these pathways. That makes it easy for you to keep thinking the same thoughts over and over without even trying.

However, the brain has "neuroplasticity," which is the ability to change its wiring, create new pathways and alter the old pathways. When you change your focus, you actually change the way information is handled in the brain and you make new pathways to carry this new information.

If you are of a negative mindset, your current neural wiring is not able to carry very high frequency positive thoughts. This is why new thoughts like *"I am amazing and Life is perfect just as it is,"* get bumped out of the system!

You cannot carry information that is dramatically different from what you have been used to thinking and believing. You must alter your wiring so that highly positive thoughts will stick and your mind will transmit the information. Your mind will not accept information it cannot neurologically integrate. You need to create new neurologic pathways that can hold this new type of information. You do this by focusing your attention on what you do want....over and over until it's automatic.

The more you practice this, the more aware you become of the things that please you, so they suddenly seem to be more abundant. Receptors in the brain shift and adjust, and your neural pathways become more adept at letting this type of information in. You begin to notice this new information everywhere because you have literally changed the type information your brain can receive. Therefore, you enhance your brain's capacity to carry this positive information the more you focus on what you *do* want.

## Rampage of Appreciation

The first time I learned this I was at the gym working out. I wasn't in a particularly good mood and was feeling sluggish on the stairstepper machine. What I wanted was to feel great and have an awesome workout...so I tried this exercise to change my state. I began by noticing some things around me that I could appreciate like the machine I was on, the cleanliness of the gym, the music that was on, and simple things around me.

At the time, I was surrounded by several television sets, put in place to go with the exercise machines. I have the habit of avoiding mainstream media and TV, as I find it contaminates my mindset in ways that work against what I want, so I was not very fond of having all of these TVs in my face. It was annoying and my energy was pretty low. I was somewhat reluctant as I began because it was hard to find things I appreciated. I was in a gym, after all! Once I started rolling though, I felt better, and better and soon it was so easy to find things I appreciated.

I appreciated the awesome exercise classes they have, the way my skin felt with the temperature in the space, my joints and how they move so easily... Suddenly I was feeling great. I became aware of how awesome it was that they had put all these TVs exactly in the right place so you could watch whatever you wanted as you workout. This thought surprised me because I really felt how true it was. It was like a miracle!

Bring your mind's attention to things that please you. This can be anything: joy over your child, awe at the sunset, that cool pair of shoes you look so cute in, or living the life of your dreams.

*Your brain does not know the difference between the real and the imagined.*

It will generate positive chemicals whether you are experiencing something you love *or just thinking about experiencing it*, and it will generate negative chemicals when you think about something you do not want.

## MindBody Prescription

Anytime you find yourself feeling unhappy, complaining, or experiencing anything you do not want, turn it around to its opposite and be aware of what you *DO* want. Just flip it! If you notice you might be late, think: "*I want to be on time.*" If you notice you're feeling fatigued, think: "*I want to feel vibrant and alert.*"

If you find yourself complaining to a friend: "*He's always late to pick me up.*" Turn this into: "*I would love for him to pick me up on time.*" Find all the ways you have been training your brain to be negative, and turn them around!

Note: Be sure to do this in a celebratory way. When we're resentfully stating: "*I want what I want!*" like a bratty two-year-old, it does not have the same effect.

Instead, simply juice your cells up with the thought:
"*I would love* ____(fill in the blank)," and let your mind come up with the details.

# Question:
### *I'm thinking positive thoughts and nothing's happening. Why isn't this working for me?*

The shifts happens immediately, but when we're in a low state, it may take some momentum before the positive chemicals will outweigh the negative, and you feel it emotionally.

Also, the neural pathways in the brain take time before they rewire. That means you have to be persistent with this practice. Once you have shifted emotionally, you are in the positive chemical state and your brain has an increased capacity to consider new ideas and beliefs. This is when new ideas will stick and you will be able to hold them. The brain then begins to handle this new information and changes in the hardwiring occur.

Persist and let this tool go to work on your body!

# Affirmation

*"I am powerful and create whatever I think about."*

*Note:*
If This is not about trying to be "positive,"
Trying to do that when you're feeling bad will
just stress you out.
I made you a great audio download about this.
They key is, DON'T try to be positive! It will
just stress you out and be counterproductive.
Here is the link:

## DrKimD.com/BePositive

# MindBody Tool #4: Use Your Words

*"Whether a man believes he can or he cannot, he is always right."*

*— Henry Ford*

## The Most Powerful Medicine

Your words are one of the most powerful creative forces you use every day. By now you understand that your thoughts affect your cells, your emotions, and all of your experiences, yet your words are even more powerful than your thoughts, because instead of just floating around in your head, they are concrete manifestations you put out into the world.

*Your words are the beliefs you hold most strongly.*

When words are spoken, whether they are true or not, your brain begins to process the information as if it were true, that's why some forms of advertising can be so powerful. Your brain absorbs the nice woman smiling on the commercial as if she were your trusted friend. She looks like your trusted friend and sounds like a reliable person, so the information gets absorbed by the brain and is accepted as true. This information can be about anything from the value of a hair product to the certainty of your financial demise. Your brain is a receptor, and the advertising industry has studied exactly what words to use to get into it. Words can make you buy into new ideas and beliefs...even at the expense of your health.

If the words you speak induce fear, you create an immediate negative chemical response. This destroys you *at the level of your cells and DNA*, and so creates the reality that you are afraid of: destruction and death.

## You Decide Who Is Right

The reason the words someone says are integrated and accepted is because on some level, you respect the person speaking them. You have in some way given power to that person. That's why when your mother tells you your hair looks a bit shabby, you're horrified; whereas when some stranger on the street says it, you shrug it off. Depending on the power we have vested in a particular person, their words are strongly integrated into our physiology.

However, there is no one, no matter how much

you respect them or how much power you deem them to have, whose words have as much power in your system as...*YOU*. According to your cells, you are the world's leading expert on everything!

*The voice that has the greatest impact on your cells is your own.*

Your cells respond chemically in a more pronounced way to your own voice than to the voice of anyone else, no matter how successful, brilliant or powerful that person is. Your brain takes you as the last word on everything. It will automatically respond to what you say as if it's absolute truth. What you speak becomes your reality. You can see then, why it is especially important to speak empowering, life-giving words that leave space for possibility.

If you are ill, every time you state: *"I feel like crap,"* or *"I'm so tired,"* or *"my fibromyalgia..."* you are affirming and recreating your state of illness. Your entire body is listening, and these words are programming it on what to do: create harmful chemicals that make you sick.

*The Truth will always make you feel better, so find it!*

The Truth in your body is always Life-filled. There is possibility in every moment and your body is meant to expand in aliveness. Therefore, find what's True (with a capitol "T") and let go of the truth (lowercase "t") that is really just your perspective. Find possibility.

A possibility-infused statement like: *"My body is processing something; I will feel better soon"* gets your message across that something significant is going on, but puts you in an empowered state. It invites your body to receive the idea that it is doing something productive and will soon be even better. It honors your body, and puts the illness in a different context. The body responds accordingly and chemical changes occur to bring about health.

## Use Affirmative Statements

Always state the positive aspect of your desire. Instead of saying: *"I have to leave so I'm not late for my appointment,"* say: *"I will get going so that I arrive on time for my appointment."* If you are already late, stay positive and state: *"My timing is perfect and elegant and I trust that all things are in order,"* or *"The Universe always works everything out for me, and this will work out too."*

Instead of stating to your friend or child: *"Be careful so you don't fall, get in an accident, trip, etc.,"* state: *"Be careful so you stay steady, arrive safely, stay healthy, etc."* These words keep the mind centered on the desired outcome. What you focus on is what you are creating, so speak what you want to create. Especially remember this with children. Children are especially vulnerable to the power of words.

When I was young I had a friend who had Type 1 Diabetes. She frequently would say *"I'm so tired"* and rub her face. She looked healthy and vibrant, but I figured that perhaps her diabetes made her feel tired all the time. Years later during high school we reconnected and I heard her saying the same thing. Over and over at random times. It had become a habit. *"I'm so tired."* This time I noticed she used it as sort of a conversation filler. When conversations would run dry, she would insert her habitual *"I'm so tired"* and rub her face. By now, she looked very run down and tired.

The power of your words applies especially to work situations, an area where so many of us are currently losing energy and health. Our work is meant to be an outlet of self-expression where we use our unique skills and talents to add value in the world. Work could be a fulfilling, joyful experience of using your strengths and talents and finding meaning in your life. For most of us today, however, it's more of an experience of being forced to do something we really don't want to do. This perspective is a victim state and it always comes with a health cost.

## How to Know When You're A Victim

You will know you've entered the victim state when you notice that you demonize your boss or coworkers for the negative experience you have in your work. Stop trying to change those around you and start changing your words! Instead of saying *"My boss is a pain and is always criticizing me,"* state: *"I'm feeling frustrated with her behavior and I choose to be treated with respect."*

This applies to any area of your life you want to change. Start by noticing and changing your words. Instead of: *"I never get what I really want,"* state: *"I would love to have more positive experiences than I have had in the past."* This honors and expresses your frustration while inviting in a new possibility.

A patient of mine had been experiencing pain in

her body, achy joints, low energy, headaches, and multiple other symptoms for years. She had seen multiple doctors by the time she found me. I asked some questions about her symptoms and she began telling me her story. The words she used were *"my pain," "my disease,"* and *"my Fibromyalgia."*

She'd been diagnosed with Fibromyalgia, a pain syndrome for which there are many causes and which most doctors find it very difficult to treat. Patients with Fibromyalgia typically experience unrelenting pain, fatigue and foggy-headedness. Many feel a sense of defeat because so many of the things they try do not make a difference in their symptoms. I've had many colleagues complain about the difficulties of treating this disease.

I happen to love addressing Fibromyalgia because the kind of work I do gets to the root causes of the symptoms, so patients with this kind of illness respond very well to the work I do. So when this patient described her symptoms I listened intently.

She went on to tell me *"Nothing ever works for me, doctor. The pain just keeps getting worse."* and *"I know there isn't much you can do to make this all go away, but maybe there's something that will help me feel better."* I listened and breathed, feeling the heaviness and despair in what she was saying. In moments like this, it can be difficult to not be overwhelmed by that despair. It feels hopeless to the patient, and can be a devastating diagnosis.

I asked her if she would be willing to consider a new possibility: *that even though her experience had been that nothing would make it better, there might be possibilities available she hadn't yet discovered.* At first she was reluctant. Her despair was so great that it was difficult for her to consider anything other than *"Nothing can be done and it's hopeless."* However, after bringing her through a process to honor her journey and integrate the despair and hopelessness that came with it, she was able to open to a whole new experience.

By the end of the visit she not only had new tools and treatments to use, she also had a new mindset that brought hope and possibility. This, more than anything else I did for her that day, would be the most powerful part of her healing.

## What Never to Say

Watch the words you use, especially when

talking about your health. Avoid using *"never,"* *"always,"* *"hate,"* *"can't stand,"* or other strongly negative words, or labeling things in a static way.

Life is always in flux. When something seems to be stuck, it is only because you have recreated it the same way over and over and over. Allow space for this in your conversation. Start by making a change in how you see it. These little tweaks in how you use your words create the life you desire by keeping you in an open, empowered place.

Life is constantly changing, and possibility abounds, so have your language reflect this and you will invite newness and joy into your life.

## MindBody Prescription

For the next one week, be mindful of your words. Choose to speak empowering words that reflect the life you would like to be living, in contrast to words that describe and reflect the one you are currently in. Instead of describing what you do not want in a certain situation, state what you DO want in your experience, and avoid using the words *"never,"* *"always,"* and *"I can't."*

When you catch yourself using your old disempowered language...start the 7 days over again! When you can do this for 7 days in a row, you have solidly established a new way of speaking for good!

# Question:
### *But I am feeling ill. Does this mean I should just lie?*

Lying generates harmful stress chemicals. This tool is not about "being positive" or "fake it until you make it." It is about using your words to create possibility that feels good, not overriding what you are feeling in an attempt to create something better. Speak the Truth of how you feel and what you want, instead of the truth of your "story."

If you have been ill for years and are frustrated and scared that nothing will help you, possibility language would be: *"I have been ill for years and none of the things I've tried before have helped, so I'm scared this won't work either. Sometimes I feel hopeless"* instead of: *"My illness is so bad that nothing ever works for me. It's hopeless."* The latter affirms the situation you do not want, while the former leaves space open for possibility while still communicating your truth.

Let the new thoughts in, even if they are not yet apparent in your reality. Begin to base your thoughts and beliefs not on what you are currently experiencing, but on what you would like to be true. Choose words that make you feel how you would like to feel.

## Affirmation
*"I speak possibility and life responds accordingly."*

# MindBody Tool #5: Ask Better Questions

*"Questions provide the key to unlocking our unlimited potential."*
— *Tony Robbins*

Your mind is unlimited, expansive and brilliant...so why hasn't it figured out the solutions to your life's challenges? It has never been asked to do so.

The mind is constantly turning its wheels and will answer any question thrown its way. It retrieves answers the way a dog will chase and retrieve a bone. The key is to ask your mind to retrieve the kind of information that assists you in creating what you want.

With all the negative media we are faced with the mind is typically racing with worries of disaster. It asks: *"What's wrong with me? Why haven't I lost weight? Why haven't I gotten my finances together? Why isn't my lover more attentive to my needs?"*

The brain delivers the answers to whatever questions you have. Therefore, your mind is filled with all the things that are wrong with you, and all the things that are not working in your life.

Since your thoughts create your internal state, this leaves you in a perpetual negative chemical state and causes mental and cellular impairment. Because your internal state is the basis for your external reality, this recreates whatever challenges you are experiencing.

If you instead, center the mind on positive and expansive questions, your brain will bring you totally different information and generate a state of inspiration. Ask yourself: *"What's the best thing about me?"* or *"What's the best thing I could do to easily get the result I want?"*

## What I Loved About Getting Dumped

This tool dramatically changed my life. I had just been dumped and felt like my world was over. My mind scrambled with trying to identify where I had gone wrong. Over and over I pieced the scenes together in my mind. There was nothing I could do. It was a done deal and I knew I had to accept it as it was. I asked: *"How is this the best thing that ever happened to me?"*

Immediately I became aware of the myriad of things in the relationship that were not a fit. Suddenly I was very clear that had we stayed together, I would never have what I most wanted. It was amazing how quickly this question brought me totally different information that inspired me and made me hugely appreciative of my situation.

Your mind is hardwired to create. Depending on the state you are in, it can create a masterpiece...or a catastrophe. Neurologic pathways are set in place and will deliver the same information over and over until you make changes in the programming. Asking better questions rewires your brain by causing the nerve synapses to connect in a different way. This changes the architecture of your brain so that it thinks differently.

*When we think differently we create an entirely different life.*

I've frequently told the story about how I reversed years of a chronic illness in just 10 days. Doctors had told me nothing could be done other than multiple medications and major lifestyle changes like stopping running and using special products to prevent triggering the illness. One of the MindBody tools I used to reverse this illness so quickly was to repattern my brain messaging.

Instead of waking up and looking for the symptoms, figuring out whether it was going to be a good or a bad day, I disciplined my mind to notice everything that was going right. I would purposefully look for reasons to be appreciative and feel good. Even when I felt like crap, I forced myself to focus on my mantra: *"I am powerfully healthy and strong."* At first this was hard work. I felt like crap and that was my whole experience, but I persisted, and within a short time it became easy to focus on the new idea. Soon, I could feel this mantra all the time. I had rewired the patterns in my brain.

Once these new neurologic pathways are set, the mind automatically generates life-giving thoughts. Without you even trying, you generate positive emotional states that energize you and drive inspired action. Use questions as a way to do this so your mind does not create resistance.

## When Affirmations Go Wrong

You must be careful with using mantras and affirmations, however. When you're feeling bad and say an affirmation like *"I'm amazing and can do anything!"* the first thing that comes to mind is how *untrue* the statement is.

The mind rebels by saying "Yeah, right!" and you may actually feel worse! Asking a question gets around this because it sort of stuns the mind, and the mind has nothing to do other than answer the question!

Listen to what happens in your mind when you ask:

*"Why is my life such a huge success?"*

*"Why am I so healthy and filled with vitality?"*

*"Why do I have so much fortune and wealth?"*

…See what I mean?

How do you feel? You just changed your brain activity and began to shift your chemistry. Your cells are beginning to be fed this nurturance and generate more energy and vitality.

*Asking better questions delivers you an inspired life.*

## The What If Game

Another great way to ask better questions is to play the "What If Game."

In this game we use "What if" questions. This is another fun way to instill the positive chemical state and create the results you want. You don't even need answers.

Just feel the response when you ask: *"What if* I were totally healthy and at peace?" *"What if* things began to come to me way more easily than I ever imagined?" *"What if* reading this book was the best thing I ever did?" *"What if* my life transforms now?" *"What if* what is being said here is true and I really can receive my deepest desires?"

Release the little voice in your head that says this is silly, this isn't working, or this is too simple to be effective. Release the old, grungy way of thinking that has been dictating your life. That's just your old programming. Let go of focusing on what hasn't changed yet and try it!

# MindBody Prescription

Every time you find yourself challenged and

you face a choice, ask:

*"What action could I take right now that would enhance my life the most?"*

If you find yourself in a negative situation you cannot change, ask:

*"How is this the best thing that has ever happened to me?"*

Then let go and let the answers come.

Set reminders to go off on your phone during your day that ask you the question:

*"Why is my life so wonderful today?"*

## Question:
***"Don't I have to figure things out? How can I get the right answers if I don't ask about my problem?"***

You don't need to figure anything out. Your mind finds the "how" automatically for you. The information you need will come to mind and move you in the right direction. All you need to do is set your mind toward your desired outcome, and life takes care of the rest.

Inspirations and solutions will become apparent when you generate thoughts that are aligned with your outcome. Stop trying to figure out how, and just allow yourself to imagine. Use questions to bring you into the state that guides you to create what it is that you want.

Remember, life gets you in action, motivates and inspires you to do or say everything that you do. Let your mind do the work to establish the motivations and inspirations that bring about what you want. It's a natural process. You can trust your higher mind.

# Affirmation

*"Why am I so vibrant and alive?"*

*"Why am I so fulfilled and happy?"*

# MindBody Tool #6: Find Your Inner Ease

*"To the mind that is still, the whole universe surrenders."*

*— Lao Tzu*

The key to this tip is tuning into your emotional state and consciously bring yourself higher. If you are feeling anxious or frustrated, whatever you do to fix the problem will not work to bring you your desired result. You must first address what's going on inside you.

You can't operate at peak performance in the stress state. You can't learn new information. You can't find solutions. You can't lose weight or create ideal health. What you want will continue to elude you, because focusing on the problem creates the negative chemical state that impairs your performance, clouds your judgment, and deteriorates your cells. *You can't use a negative mind to create a positive situation.*

## First, Change Your Mind

Let's say you want to lose weight and get fit.

You feel frustrated with your body because you think it's too fat, too flabby, unattractive and inadequate. The negative chemical state created by your negative thoughts increases cortisol and the stress hormones, which impairs your body's ability to burn off fat. Even if you force yourself through your workout and are able to put in a solid hour, the stress state you generate with your self-criticism works against you chemically, and your body will resist losing weight.

The same thing occurs when you try to work harder to get ahead. When you push yourself to overwork even though you are tired and frustrated, the work you do will be ineffective and inefficient. The negative chemical state of frustration impairs your brain function, making it impossible to see the big picture, come up with creative solutions and tap into insight and inspired thinking.

*You cannot win in the fight against your own body.*

Often, I do my best work after taking a break to exercise or take a nap. Things flow effortlessly, and it takes me a fraction of the time to complete something. I find ease and even joy in something I was previously struggling with.

When I am frustrated and shift my internal state *first*, my actions and efforts will successfully bring about my desired result.

This works for anything and anytime you are having distress. Find your inner ease by gifting yourself a hot bath, a nap, a walk, a personal pep talk, or even just a few deep restorative breaths. (Remember what you learned in MindBody Tool #2? You will get so good at it that it takes seconds to create a shift!)

## Life Reflects the Stress You Carry

Sometimes we're so sold on working toward an outcome that we won't stop no matter how much resistance we're having. I've seen this with many people who do things "the hard way," and will adamantly tell you why they have to keep going and things can't be easy. Sometimes we fear what will happen if we stop; we think the world will fall apart.

I had a patient who was so stressed with managing her family duties, her career and caring for her home that her health suffered terribly. She became anxious and depressed and developed Chronic Fatigue Syndrome. Her doctor prescribed an antidepressant and she came to me because she felt there had to be a better way to manage this.

When I reviewed her case, it was clear she was putting everyone else first and not taking adequate care of herself. *"But I have to do all of this,"* she defended, *"I can't just let my kids starve!"* She was convinced that if she stopped holding everything together that nothing would get done. What she failed to see in this stress state was that she had multiple untapped resources, such as a partner, her husband, who deeply wanted her to be happy and healthy.

As we began our work together, and she incorporated the MindBody tools, she was able to see that old resentments toward her husband had been keeping her from letting him contribute to her life. She became aware of all the ways he had attempted to support her while she downplayed his contribution. Finally, he had given up.

She began to laugh when she awakened to all the ways she had devised the roles for everyone in her household. She was the martyr who worked her butt off and everyone else was the ungrateful receivers who took her for granted. She revealed that she had even been secretly resenting her own children!

They were all following her lead, which was based on her belief that she should come last. As a result, she simply hadn't asked anyone for support.

In the stress state, she was convinced she was alone and taken advantage of by her family, but in her "right mind" it was clear that she, herself, had created all of this. The empowerment that came with this awakening was enough for her to reverse her symptoms (and her chronic illness) within a month.

Release guilt, fear, or whatever resistance you have to stopping and doing these things that make you feel whole. When you notice you are carrying resistance of any kind, be willing to do whatever will bring you into a more peaceful inner state. Do it in the moment you catch yourself so you don't accumulate this energy over time and become ill (or just age faster!)

## Finding Inner Ease In Traffic

I was driving on the highway on my way to an appointment. For some reason there was tons of traffic, and I began to get that sinking feeling that comes when I know I'm going to be late. I was bummed...but I was aware!

I was totally aware of feeling bummed out, thinking that I should have taken the alternative route I usually take, that I should have left earlier, and that I really should be better about being on time. I began wishing I were like those perfect people in my head who are always on time, and started thinking that I was a total loser for not planning better and leaving sooner.

As I became aware of the way I was feeling (and all of these ridiculous thoughts), I brought my attention to my feelings of dread and anxiety, and I took a few deep breaths. I began to remember something I had learned from a brilliant spiritual teacher of mine, Esther Hicks:

*The only important thing to do is feel good.*

I told myself that it would somehow be okay that I was late. Maybe I wasn't meant to be on time and that something even better would happen. I also considered that perhaps there was just an obstruction ahead and this would all clear so maybe I'd be moving soon – and I felt a bit better. I told myself that everything happens in perfect order, and I remembered that things always have worked out for me in the past, even when I didn't understand how they possibly could.

I sat in the traffic, but now was almost totally at peace. Just as this peaceful feeling began to sink in the traffic started flowing a little better and a little better and a little better, until within a minute I was up to full speed. There was no obstruction, construction, or accident on the road, just the sudden flow of traffic exactly at the point where I began to generate peace!

This is how the process of clearing up our internal space works to clear up our external environment. Not only was I not late as I had initially begun to anticipate, but I arrived at my appointment three minutes early! I experienced ease in my life situation because I let go of my expectation and connected with inner ease.

I'm not saying that you will move traffic with your thoughts and emotions or that things will suddenly begin to go exactly the way you want them to. I'm saying that when you bring yourself into the state of inner ease, life will sort itself out in a way that reflects that ease and ultimately serves you. Sometimes that occurs in ways that don't make sense (like my story on getting dumped I told you about earlier!). You may not think things are going the way they're supposed to, but I guarantee that if you are in a higher emotional state, it's only a matter of time before you begin to experience your world in a better way.

## Inner Ease During An Argument

This works like magic when you are in an argument with your spouse.

Get present, breathe, and find your inner ease in the moment no matter what is happening. Stop defending and release your resistance. You will immediately stop generating the negative chemicals that are clouding your judgment and preventing you from seeing the big picture. You will also stop the toxic communication coming from your body that is contributing to your spouse (or whoever you are in conflict with) being so contracted and shut down. Inevitably, your heightened emotional state will allow you to stop your portion of the chaos.

You will gain insight and be able to consider the other's point of view. Often this is the exact thing that is most needed in the moment: the ability to understand the other person's perspective without defending yourself or accusing them of being wrong.

I can't tell you how many times this tool has saved my marriage…and made it even better! It wasn't always evident immediately, but with practice, I've now been able to instantly dissolve any conflict that comes up before it turns into an argument.

## MindBody Prescription

The next time you are in a negative state or you are experiencing a situation you do not want, ask yourself:

*"What it is that I most need right now?"*
(It may be love, rest, or physical comfort.)

Then, imagine how it would feel to receive it.

Hold that feeling in your body for several breaths and receive it. See it coming into your body with the inhale breaths. Continue to breathe this way until you feel a shift in how you feel.

## Question:
*"How do I find ease when I'm feeling really, really bad?"*

When you are feeling bad, so much of your

attention goes onto what you do not want and it generates more negative, harmful chemicals that contribute to the toxicity you are experiencing. It can be challenging to break this cycle and feel better.

Finding inner ease seems impossible, and *trying to feel better brings resistance, so you end up feeling worse!* (I can't tell you how many patients I've treated with depression, chronic pain and low energy due to this exact cycle!!)

At times like these, there's only one direction to go towards, and that's deeper down into the negative emotion. It's like a process of surrender.

First, you have to notice that you are feeling bad. If you can bring your thoughts to what you *do* want or to the opposite of what's going on, that will change things up, but sometimes the problem is just too overwhelming and in your face!

*When the resistance is too big, simply embrace the pain.*

That's right, embracing and allowing is actually a positive chemical state, even if it is unwanted pain that we are embracing! If I'm angry, I'll shout: *"I'm so freaking angry!"* (Sometimes just in my head.) If I'm scared, I'll just lean into how scared I really am and take a few breaths. I bring all of my attention to the pain to really feel it. This always dissipates the negativity and gets me to a state that feels better.

What you're doing here is bringing all of your attention onto the "unwanted" thing. Use your breath to focus your mind. This actually releases resistance to it because while you feel it, you're not thinking about it! You stop your ideas about it. You stop your fears about it. You stop your story about it. *You just feel it.* Then, it stops being a "scary monster that could destroy me" and instead becomes just a pure emotion.

## Affirmation

*"I stay centered in ease, and life works out the details to support me."*

DrKimD.com/Resources

Kim D'Eramo, D.O.

# MindBody Tool #7: Be Clear of Your Ultimate Outcome

*"Whatever the mind of man can conceive and believe, it can achieve."*
*— Napoleon Hill*

Your brain is like the most brilliantly designed machine ready to serve you in any way in every moment. When you do not take advantage of this, it's like having a Lear jet with autopilot capabilities to fly you wherever you want to go... and using it for local access as you steer it up and down the same street manually.

While your conscious mind has access to a very limited amount of information, your higher mind is infinite. Your mind has access to more information than you could possibly imagine. Your expansive mind knows things from the square root of 42 to the best place for you to go for dinner tonight in order to have the most fun. So how do you tap into your mind's expansive capabilities?

*Be clear of your ultimate outcome.*

What exactly is it that you want in life? In a relationship? In your career? In your finances? What does your ideal life look like?

## Setting Your True North

Your mind is your guidance system and you must set the compass. When you enter in your exact destination by getting clear, your mind guides you in creating it. When you get your mind focused clearly on exactly what you want, this sets your internal GPS to your desired destination.

Your mind is constantly taking orders and creating based on what you think about. The thing is, you've been all over the place with your focus and instruction!

One minute you may think: *"I want a fabulous lover and a lifelong partnership,"* and the next moment you think: *"There are no good men out there."* Maybe you think: *"I want a fabulous career with lots of money,"* then you think: *"Money doesn't grow on trees."* Your mind delivers your experience according to the information you tell it. It will always present you with information and experiences to prove you right.

You are programming your brain on what kind of information to deliver. This is just like turning the dial on your radio and receiving different music. All of the radio waves for the different radio channels are surrounding you now. You cannot see them, but they are all there simultaneously. So it is with the information the brain is delivering to you. It depends on the way the networks in your brain are set up. You train your mind to pick up a certain frequency of information depending on what you program it to receive.

When you program your brain for the outcome you want, your neural pathways shift and your brain sets an internal map to deliver your end result. It's like a program set up to point you in the right direction in every moment. Your mind moves you into action by inspiring and motivating you. You give it the information it needs to know what you want to move toward. You must, however, be clear!

When you are clear of your ultimate outcome, you aren't confused in your choices. You give your mind the information it needs and it moves you into action. Then, things start to happen very quickly that get your life aligned with that goal.

*To the degree that you're clear, choices are effortless.*

You may be inspired to go to a certain coffee shop, where you meet exactly the person who can assist you with your business endeavor, or perhaps you suddenly think of an old friend and call him, only to find that he was in need of your support.

When you set your mind clearly on your ultimate outcome, your inner drives will motivate you and inspire you to act and behave in ways that bring about this end result. It changes the information you notice and alters what you pay attention to.

## Designing Your Life

When I wanted to create a life partnership, I used this tool avidly. I had already been through a ton of challenge in my relationships, so I finally decided to get completely clear on what exactly I wanted in my ideal mate. That way I would clearly recognize him when he showed up in my life, and I would stop fooling myself when someone showed up who was clearly not my ideal mate.

I made a list with three columns. In the left

column, I listed the *"Must Haves."* These were items I would absolutely not do without. After all the relationships I'd been through, I had really come to know myself and my desires. I was clear on my absolutes and I knew I fully deserved them! I listed things like: compassionate, kind, loving, authentic, available, financially secure, wants to be married and have kids, and completely committed to and in love with me.

In the middle column, I listed the *"It Would Be Nice Ifs."* These were items I was excited about, but knew would not be deal breakers if they were not there, like: "likes sushi and is a fabulous skier."

In the last column I listed my *"Absolutely Nots."* These were the red-flag items that I was completely clear I would not accept under any circumstances. I appreciated all of my negative experiences for teaching me what they were, and listed: "uses drugs, lies, smokes, spends money he doesn't have, and has no clear sexual boundaries."

I put the list aside and skipped about life enjoying meeting new people, and dating, because I wasn't busy thinking about whether I could make something work for the long term. I was already clear. I began having so much fun! I connected with people authentically because I had no hidden agenda going on in the back of my mind. I stayed clear and just showed up to enjoy my wonderful self.

Less than four months later I met my now-husband. He is absolutely everything I had imagined and so much more! (...and he is also an amazing skier!)

I call this process the "Design Your Life Worksheet" and use it when I coach patients and clients to get them clear on what they need and want.

## MindBody Prescription

Create a list for an area where you want transformation in your life. Describe your ideal ultimate outcome. Get clear on what is a "Must Have," an "It Would Be Nice If," and an "Absolutely Not" for you.

Then, make a commitment to this list. Let nothing be more important to you. This list is your heart. It is your personal desire and is unique and special. Do not compromise on this list for anything!

(Note, if at a later date you change your mind, that's fine. As more experience comes, you may change some of the items or move them around. Just be sure to be honest with yourself, and recommit to the updated list before you commit to anyone or anything else.)

*Option: Create a list for every area of your life- relationship, career, finances, health, home, social, and commit to your desired result for each of these areas.*

## Question:
**"What if I do not know the exact job I want or the specifics of what I want in life?"**

Even when you are not clear of the details, you can be very clear of the things that are most important to you. Let's say you want a career where you're thriving, making plenty of money, enjoying yourself, and doing what you are best at and love to do. Would it matter specifically what you are doing? If there are other factors that are important to you like prestige, respect, and independence, add them to your list. This is your design! It's actually helpful not to have too many specifics, just be totally clear on what you do know is important.

*Important!!*

Always add to your list: *"This or something even better!"* to get your mind centered on the idea of greater possibilities than what you can conceive of right now. This affects your mind and keeps you open to even greater possibility.

## Affirmation

*"Life is on my side. Everything is always working out in my favor."*

I've created a special "Design Your Life" Worksheet for you. You can get yours by visiting:

DrKimD.com/DesignYourLife

# MindBody Tool #8: Love Yourself

*"I finally realized that being grateful to my body was key to giving more love to myself."*

*— Oprah Winfrey*

Love is the most powerful force in the universe. It heals illness, feeds the poor, and gets people to do outlandish things like drive for endless hours or fly across the country weekly. Love cures illness and gives people super-human levels of strength. If you are yearning for a fulfilling life of vitality, and don't have it, chances are you could use more love in your life.

You may imagine this love coming from outside yourself and envision an ideal lover or soulmate, who will bring this love to you, only to find yourself continually disappointed that you are not getting the love you want. I can feel your pain, because I too, have searched for love outside myself and been devastatingly heartbroken.

Life doesn't work that way in love or in any other area. Your external life is a representation of your internal state. It's a mirror. Especially in relationships.

*The love you experience, you invite in through loving yourself.*

When you create love by loving yourself, you are a magnet for love. You will find that when you cultivate love for yourself, others are drawn to you. You are treated with kindness and respect, and people who don't honor you no longer show up in your life. This happens because others are affected by your field. The electromagnetic field of your body extends beyond your physical self. Your communication is directly impacting them. This goes for family and friends, and also coworkers and clients. Love harmonizes every area of your body and life.

## Make Love In Your Body

Love is not just a noun, it is also a verb. To receive it, it's a matter of giving it...*to yourself.* We've all been taught to give love to others in order to receive love ourselves, but the *bigger* truth is that the only love you have to give is the love inside you. When you limit the love you have for yourself (or put it on hold until you've lost 20 pounds), you simply don't have enough love to really give to anyone else.

When you love yourself, you generate positive chemicals that make your cells thrive. Endorphins, oxytocin, acetylcholine and antioxidants increase, making you feel energized, calm and content. This inspires you to behave in ways that attract others and invite connection. You always experience loving relationships when you first love yourself!

The emotion of love has a powerful impact on your body, and the function of your organs. Studies at the Institute of Heart Math have shown that when a person feels love, their heart beats more regularly, their breathing smooths out, and their blood pressure normalizes. Likewise, when they are in a lower emotional state like anger, the opposite happens. Their heart beat, respirations and blood pressure showed erratic changes. They also showed that the impact of a person's emotional state could be detected up to 8-10 feet away from the physical body.

*Your thoughts and emotions have impact.*

The thoughts you have about your body create your physical form. So when you think: *"Ugh, my thighs are so flabby..."* or some such critical thought, your thighs are listening and will continue to form in that way. Any negative thought you have about your body will diminish the Life Force and vitality flowing to that area.

So instead, send LOVE. That's right, even to your "less-than-perfect" bum. Start with the parts of your body that are easier to appreciate. Maybe you have beautiful eyelashes, smooth cheeks, cute knees that bend easily, or two arms to reach out and hug someone. Send love. Say: "I love you" to your symmetrical shoulders or cute toes.

Then move on to areas you currently judge to be less-than-stellar. Say hello to your wide calves in a new way. Find something you appreciate about them. I was once asked to write an ode to my thighs and it changed my relationship with them forever!

## Networks of Love

When you bring your focus to any part of your body, you bring about change to the chemistry in that area of the body. You fire up the nerves that connect to that area and bring new information into your spinal cord. If you use loving, positive attention, this works to heal a sprained ankle or to generate glow in your cheeks.

The area in the brain that corresponds to that body part lights up with increased activity. Awareness of an injured area while feeling the emotion of love actually decreases inflammation, cellular toxicity and tissue damage. This enhances healing and restores normal function to the area.

Your loving attention to an area of your body causes the sensory nerve receptors in that area to have enhanced sensitivity. There is more blood flow to that area, which means improved nutrient and oxygen delivery and improved removal of waste products and lymphatic fluid. Inflammation clears and health is enhanced. Your body will feel better and will also function better. Cells regain health and your body becomes more youthful.

## Why Hatred Causes Pain and Wrinkles

When you bring negative attention to a body part, the opposite occurs.

Pain sensitivity is enhanced and you propagate a pain cycle at the level of your spinal cord. Vessels constrict, which causes decreased nutrient and oxygen delivery to the cells and increased buildup of waste products. The pH (that's the acid-base balance) of the tissues is decreased and muscles go into spasm. Ageing and cellular degeneration are accelerated and tissues sag and wrinkle.

This is how the parts of your body that you do not like end up becoming more displeasing.

*Your cells are literally listening to your every thought about them and are responding accordingly.*

Giving your body attention in the positive state of love and appreciation makes your cells sing with vibrance and vitality. The affect spreads to clear up the "inflammatory war" that's wreaking havoc on your cells.

Whenever I catch myself looking at a part of my body with any judgment, I override all lesser thoughts by gently saying: "I love you, I love you, I love you," until I take my attention away from it. I know negative attention will only cause discord in my body, and that would create what I do not want.

Loving myself helped my body heal remarkably fast from a C-section; I required no pain medications after the surgery besides ibuprofen.

It also prevents me from getting blemishes.

I used to have little breakouts around my mouth and chin from touching my face during the day. Now, whenever I scratch my face and hear that thought coming up, I say an inner *"I love you,"* with my attention on this area. I gently say it until I literally feel this override the concerning thoughts. I haven't had a blemish like that in years.

If it's difficult to love your body, just start with appreciation. Appreciate that you have the ability to read this book! Your magnificent body allows you to do so much in the world. It even digests non-food items you may be trying to feed it with. It is your greatest ally. Give it a break from critical mind banter and begin to send it the appreciation it deserves.

## MindBody Prescription

Bring your awareness and attention to whatever area has been beat down by your judgment and mentally say: *"I love you"* over and over. Think of it as erasing years of criticism and let your cells drink it in.

Say *"I love you"* every time you look in the

mirror. Do it any time you stop at a traffic light. Do it when you take a shower. Touch those areas and send love.

If you have an especially challenged body image or an injured body part, do this while looking in the mirror for several minutes a day. This will transform your relationship with your body, and also dramatically change your health.

## Question:
*"How do I love something that I find unacceptable? Won't I just keep recreating that thing I don't want?"*

It can seem like holding disdain for your overweight body will motivate you to lose weight, but withholding love only makes things worse. (If it worked you would not be reading this book!) That's because unloving attention literally starves your body from life force.

Your natural state is one of vibrant health. Appreciation brings vitality to every area of your body and mind, even if you are certain there is nothing good about the way you are. As you open to appreciation, you will begin to perceive things in a new way. This will bring enhanced vitality to whatever your loving attention is placed upon, and generate changes in the body that bring you joy.

The energy of loving attention creates positive change.

Let it work on you.

## Meditation

Visualize a warm golden light coming into your body through the top of your head and filling your entire body. Focus especially on areas where there is pain or injury and let this golden light infiltrate that area fully.

# MindBody Tool #9: Say "Yes" to Your YESes

*"If one advances confidently in the direction of his dreams, and endeavors to live the life which he has imagined, he will meet with a success unexpected in common hours."*
— *Henry David Thoreau*

Your passions generate a sense of aliveness and vitality within you that is the elixir of life and the fountain of youth. Your passions- the things that you care most about, and love to engage in, put you in the positive chemical state whether you are doing them...or just thinking about them.

## The Best Kept Secret In Medicine

Did you know people who live a life filled with passion live approximately a decade longer, are more successful, and have a better quality of life than those who do not? According to a study at Stanford University, people who had the greatest financial success and were the happiest all noted that the most important thing they based their decisions on was: PASSION. Not finances, not logic, not practicality, *not what others expected from them.*

They were thriving because they made their choices based on what they were most passionate about doing.

What if you lived your life in accordance with that which inspires you most? How would you feel getting up every morning? What would your relationships look like? How would your body feel? How motivated would you be to be doing your daily routine?

Why aren't you making this the most important thing in your life???

So many of the people who come to me are unhappy and unhealthy because they are out of alignment with this very important piece. They spend the better part of their day doing things that do not give them much (if any) energy and inspiration, and then do all kinds of things in an attempt to feel better. They are overworked, beat-down, exhausted and depressed.

*All the medication in the world will not make up for the depletion that comes from a life void of passion.*

When you have a life without passion, you are

constantly putting more energy into things than you get out of them. You generate more metabolic waste and toxicity than your body has the resources to clear up.

When you do what you are passionate about, the opposite occurs. You open to receiving vast amounts of energy, so you feel vitalized. Doing what you are passionate about, or even just thinking about doing it, increases endorphins, antioxidants and oxytocin and you feel good. It also brings about changes in your neurotransmitters that allows you to receive information and awareness that you would not otherwise have.

## Passion Increases Productivity

When you connect with your passion, you become more efficient and effective. Your brain is more focused and it is easy to get things done. Companies where employees are supported to live their passion grow faster and establish themselves more solidly. Starbucks' philosophy of connecting workers to create a space of passion is one of the main reasons they continue to grow year after year.

What you prioritize will get most of your attention and your energy. You are literally living for the things you put first. To have spectacular health, you want your body to run efficiently. The most important thing you can do is to set up your life in alignment with the things that are most important to you; the things you care about and would give your life for.

*You give your life away to the things you prioritize.*

That is what you are doing: giving your life. Time, energy, effort and attention direct the forces of your life. You are already giving your life away to something. Whether that is something that really fuels you or not will determine your level of vitality. If you're prioritizing things you don't really care about and are willing to die for, you won't get that energy back! Be willing and committed to give your life to your passions, and your body will reap the rewards.

## How Do You Identify Your Passions?

Your passions may be things like "feeling healthy and fit," "spending quality time with family," or "enjoying wealth and prosperity."

They may be more specific things like: "designing websites," "gardening," or "coaching soccer." Your passion is anything that makes your heart sing.

I call prioritizing your passions *"Saying 'Yes' to Your YESes."* In my courses, I emphatically teach that our inner drives and deepest yearnings are the key to ideal health and great success. It is our inner YES that points us in the direction of inspiration.

When you are in your natural state of vitality, you intuitively follow this feeling and make the choices that resonate with it. Why wouldn't you? When you're connected and filled with Life Force, you always do what fuels and nurtures you. You don't compromise out of guilt or fear. If you're trying to complete a task and not getting anywhere, but are yearning for a hot bath, a long walk, a nap, or a break with a friend, take it! Sometimes it only takes a few minutes, but this reboot in productivity can dramatically decrease the time it takes to get something done.

## Why Kinda Is Not Good Enough

Your inner YES is not ambiguous. When you feel it, you *know* it. It's the *"Yahoooo!"* feeling you initially get when you consider something that sounds really good. It may not last long because it is often followed by a: *"Yeah, but...(*fill in the limiting, fear-based belief that drowns out your inner YES)*"*.

The fear-based belief may look like: *"That would never work out,"* or *"Who the heck am I to think I can do that?"* or *"That is ridiculous!"* The limiting thought may even try to confuse you with doubt by saying: *"I don't really know what I want."* You DO! It just jumped out as a feeling of vast excitement that looked completely ridiculous and irrational! That's your passion calling.

The Stanford research I mentioned earlier consistently showed that true happiness and wellbeing did not come from following the "rules" as we have been taught: study hard, get a good job, work your tail off and you'll be all set. Not only will you clearly *not* be "all set" but you won't even be remotely okay. Most people trying to retire today have had to add another decade or so to their workdays.

Most people who follow this prescription do not enjoy what they do, and suffer immense health consequences. Even if financial abundance follows, the misery associated with a life devoid of passion leads to expensive addictions, expensive medical bills and expensive divorces.

People who follow these "rules" are miserable. None of the highly successful people I've ever studied, or who were cited in the above study lived life according to this traditional model.

What creates a life of vitality and health is being true to yourself. Be true to your passion. Your inner YES guides you there. Listen every day and be willing to follow and say: *"yes"* to your YES! It is your aliveness and your ticket to vitality. Your YES is your internal GPS that guides you to your thriving life.

Follow your passion and choose what most deeply serves you. Every time you have a choice of any kind, ask yourself, *"What am I most excited about?"*

*Feel for your inner YES and follow it.*

Know that you are free to make any choice you desire. Make passion-based choices and create a life that sustains you, where you get to be who you really are, live your truth and express your authentic self. This always leads to the rejuvenation, inspiration, chance meetings, or a totally new path that is the fastest road to your success.

# MindBody Prescription

Ask yourself: "Now that I am living my ideal life, I am _____." Fill in the blank with actions you would be doing if you were in your ideal life.

Put down all the things that come to mind, then choose your favorites and write them on 3x5 index cards. Place them where you will be reminded several times daily. This keeps your attention on your passions and repeatedly boosts your energy.

## Question:
*"How can I just do what I want all the time? Don't I need to compromise and serve others in order to make life work?"*

Compromise will never make your life work. You are in the driver's seat and every time you compromise yourself, you buy into something that will not serve you. When you do this it generates stress chemicals in your body.

The urge to compromise comes from a fear-based belief that who you are is not enough. This is a negative thought and is life-depleting. The Truth is, you can have the life you desire *just for being you.* Honoring your own unique passions is the greatest service you can do for everyone you care about.

When you are in the inspired state of passion, you have greater awareness of the unity of all people, and have more compassion, understanding and love for others. Living your passion is your greatest gift to the world.

## Affirmation
*"When faced with a choice, I choose in favor of my passions!"*

DrKimD.com/Resources

# MindBody Tool #10: BE – DO – HAVE

*"If we could change ourselves, the tendencies in the world would also change. As a man changes his own nature, so does the attitude of the world change towards him."*
— *Mahatma Gandhi*

I've come across this formula in multiple teachings on success, spelled out or implied. It is the no-fail, tried and true, secret to success that all masters use and which most of us get completely backwards.

I have applied it in my own life and it always works. I've experienced work I love, friends I adore, an amazing life-partner and family of my own, and beautiful places to live every time I've desired to move.

## The No-Fail Formula

What I've done is learn how to embody what I desire to *Be*, even when life does not reflect that back to me. That means if I want to be healthy and fit, I must first enter the mindset of a healthy, fit person. This happens *before* the weight is lost or the illness is gone.

If I want to be adored and cherished by my partner, I must *first* embrace the beliefs and ideas of a person who is adored and cherished, such as "*I am worthy of love and belonging.*"

This first part of the equation is the most important. *Be*ing happy or anything else, can only happen Now, not in the future, and it can only happen when you choose to *Be* it.

> *What works unfailingly in attracting your heart's desire is: Be-Do-Have.*

Once you are able to *Be* happy, and choose it despite the circumstances, you shift immediately into the positive chemical state. This state drives all of your actions and behaviors.

You get inspiration and vitality so you can sustain your work and your workout! Your brain works better so everything occurs to you differently. You have more positive insights and see the best traits in other people, which they respond positively to. You therefore, bring out the best in others. The things you are inspired and energized to *Do* will create support for the positive emotional state you are in.

## We've Been Given the Wrong Remedy

We've been taught by society that the key to happiness and success is to attain stuff, achieve stuff, or get stuff. Once you *Have* that, you will be able to *Do* what you want, and *then* you will *Be* happy. The stuff may be a nice house, a job, marriage, a certain amount of money, a certain number of children, your ideal body weight...or any number of things you think will make you happy. You may be completely convinced that once you have attained this thing you will then be fulfilled!

*The Have-Do-Be equation doesn't work.*

Maybe you can't even imagine being happy and fulfilled without these qualifications being met. This is only because of your beliefs. Maybe you don't feel worthy of just *Being* happy for no reason. Maybe you don't feel you've done enough to deserve to be completely happy. Perhaps you don't think it's possible to just *Be* happy without having achieved or attained these items first (or worse, you think it's selfish to do that!).

All of these are just beliefs. Even if they are based on your experiences, they are still just beliefs. These experiences have you convinced that you absolutely need to first *Have* a certain thing in order to *Be* happy. You may be so convinced of this, you work in a job you don't enjoy, hold off on dating someone you're really psyched about, or spend years pursuing goals that are not your true passions...all at the expense of your health.

When you focus on the *Have,* and then *Do* what you think you should be doing in order to then *Be* what you want, it's a compromise. You are not living in a state of vitality and aliveness.

Let's say John wants to have a nice home and a happy family. He's been taught to study hard and get a good education, so he can get a good job, pay for a home, and provide for his family. What he really wants to do is create art and travel around the world, but instead he goes to school. He does this because he thinks it will bring him all of the things he wants even though his heart isn't in it.

Ten years later John works 60 hours a week, rarely exercises, and hardly sees his family. He has anxiety, high blood pressure, and pre-diabetes because he's been living in a negative chemical state. There's tension in his marriage because John doesn't know how to connect with others. He isn't, after all, connected with himself. He's doing a life he doesn't really want to do. Life is empty when we do it according to *Have-Do-Be*.

Because John is empty and without real aliveness, when it comes time for his company to restructure, John is laid off. Now he has no job, no money, and no happy family.

*You can't create a vibrant body and an inspired life if you are not inspired.*

Life doesn't work according to the *Have-Do-Be* equation, because when inspiration is missing, it's just an empty life. That's why even when you get all of the things you think you must *Have*, you are ultimately unfulfilled. All the beautiful homes in the world will not bring you what you are looking for, and all the antidepressants in the world will not make you feel fulfilled.

When you go after having things because you think they will bring you a desired end result, there is no passion to drive your actions. When you do life according to the *Have-Do-Be* equation, it never generates true fulfillment and vitality. Never.

# Why You Can't Just *Have* It

There are three reasons why this will never work. One is that you can never experience happiness, peace or any kind of fulfillment when it is based in the *future*. Happiness can only exist now because life occurs in the present.

*Your body only exists in this moment.*

There is no other moment. (If you don't believe me, try to find one!)

The second reason the *Have-Do-Be* equation doesn't work is because when you make your happiness contingent on having something external -whether that is an item, an achievement, or a number on the scale- your happiness is *conditional*. It will always be linked to the fear of losing that thing. True happiness, peace, or thriving is generated within, is *unconditional*, and cannot be taken away.

The third reason the *Have-Do-Be* approach doesn't work is because your *life always reflects your internal state*. When you go after things you are not truly passionate about just because you think they will bring you happiness, you are not in the positive chemical state. Unless what you are *Do*ing is derived out of *Be*ing in the state of *joy, passion and appreciation*, your actions will not bring you more joy, passion or appreciation!

The happiness and satisfaction that come from attaining a goal are limited and fleeting unless they are derived from a state of joy and happiness. When you are first *Be*ing happy (or successful, fulfilled, worthy), all the circumstances to support it come flooding into your life. They can't *not* come into your experience. Then you *Have* that which supports your positive state of *Be*ing.

Instead of being a grind, life becomes a joy. When you do life according to the *Be-Do-Have* equation, your actions and behaviors are easy to maintain, because your inner state of *Be*ing supports them. "Work" becomes effortless, and having what you want is an inevitable result.

## How Do I *Be*?

It's a bit counterintuitive to take your attention off of what you're *Do*ing, and put it onto how you're *Be*ing. It requires you to be aware of your inner state so you know what's driving your actions (and therefore, what result they will create). Practicing the Instant Elevation Tool from earlier in this book will help you master this quickly.

Another challenge I've had patients ask is: *"How am I going to get anything done?!"* In this culture that's so action-oriented, it can seem like putting all of your attention on *Be*ing won't accomplish anything. How can you get anything done if you're just focusing *Be*ing all the time? That's where the counterintuitive part comes in. When you truly fire up an inner state of inspiration, you can't *not* get into inspired action.

Now, that won't likely look like the busy action so many millions of Americans live in. You'll actually come out of busy-ness entirely. Inspired action is directed, focused, purposeful, and highly impactful…and sometimes it looks like doing nothing. You're not going to have anyone giving you kudos for that.

Unlike action that stems from the *"I have to Have it"* mentality, the inspired action of *Be-Do-Have* doesn't always look productive. Sometimes your inspired action is to stop everything and just sit in stillness. Sometimes it's fierce motion that's called for. Inspired action is balanced. More often, however, your actions will look just like what others are busy doing to try to get results...except they will work.

Imagine what you desire -a slim fit body, money, success, freedom, loving partnership...and feel what it would be like to have that now. Feel how it feels to live that experience in your body. You will begin to generate endorphins, oxytocin, antioxidants, and other positive chemicals *just by thinking about this!* You also shift your brain into an expansive, winning mindset. This gives you energy, motivation and inspiration.

## What Do I *Do*?

What would you be doing if you were already a huge success? What choices would you make? How would you stand, walk, speak? How would you move if you were loved beyond measure? What would you look like if you were happy, healthy, and fulfilled right now?

Your physiology (chemical state) is deeply dependent on your posture and your movements. Even the way you stand impacts your internal state! Standing in a slumped position with shoulders hunched and head hanging low makes it impossible to harbor joyful, happy, vibrant thoughts. In contrast, standing erect, shoulders back and head held high makes it *inevitable* that you hold thoughts of empowerment, strength and joy.

Even the simple act of smiling induces a state of happiness by increasing hormones that initiate this state. Try looking up, smiling as hard as you can for ten seconds, then try to feel depressed. You can't!

So get yourself into a higher state of *Being,* then *Do* whatever it is you are inspired to do. The right actions naturally emanate from your state of *Be*ing. You won't have to think about it. In fact, *don't think about it.* You will only interfere.

## Your Body Says It All For You

Ninety-three percent of the communication you give off is below the level of conscious thinking. Your inner state of *Be*ing comes across in your voice: your tone, volume, pace, and pauses. It is expressed through your body language: posture and movements. It also comes across in your physiology: the subtle but powerful electromagnetic field of your body has an impact on everything around you.

You can't possibly calculate all of this. It is conducted by your body's wisdom and alignment with your state of *Be*ing. All of these communications convey your worth and your value…and *everyone around you receives these messages.*

This is why you can have all the right credentials and still not get the job. If inside you are thinking "I have no idea what I'm doing; don't hire me!" that message comes across loud and clear during the interview. This is also why many wonderful and deserving women repeatedly attract men who mistreat them. When we hold the belief "I'm not worthy," others eventually get the message.

*Life will always reflect what's going on in your mind.*

Using the *Be-Do-Have* equation is the key to generating the power you need to create the energy and life you really want. Learn and practice improving your state of *Be*ing.

## Having Comes Naturally

From this heightened state you will *Have* the life circumstances consistent with staying in that state. Because your *Do*ing stems from a heightened state of *Be*ing, you create an effect that supports you.

People treat you differently, new opportunities open up to you, and relationships are smooth and connected. Your physiology responds positively so you will create a more fit, vibrant, healthy body. Put your energy and attention on the *Be*, and *Hav*ing becomes automatic.

## MindBody Prescription

Act as if. Embody your end result:

-Stand as if you were a great success.

-Walk and move as though you were deeply loved and cherished.

-Speak as though you had great security and deep peace.

Hold that feeling in your body for several breaths and receive it. Breathe this way until you feel an emotional shift inside.

Do this any time you feel insecure or have anxiety over your ability to create your desired outcome.


# Question:

*"If I just decide to be happy now, exactly as I am, won't I lose all motivation to make a change? It's not really okay for me to stay this way."*

Starting with your state of *Be*ing does not mean you don't get into action to create a new result. It just creates a new foundation for your actions. When you start with *Be*ing that which you want, you *allow the power of your body* to generate change, instead of continuing your ineffective actions.

We're socialized to think that staying in action is the only way to generate progress. As I've laid out here, that there's more to it than that. *The energy of your body itself has impact,* even if you're just sitting there. This may take a little faith at first before you see that this works, because it can seem that by halting our actions to address our inner state, things may fall apart. Maybe for years you've been told to work hard to *Have* security, and once you have it, then you can *Do* what you really want to do. Maybe you believe that you will finally *Be* happy once you meet a romantic partner.

*Release your ideas about how life works.*

You have been running a rat race. Security, peace, love or any other state you desire comes from *within* and is available to you now. The only thing life can offer is support for the internal state you have cultivated. Try it, then look for evidence of life responding.

# Affirmation

*"I am safe and secure in the power of my own inner knowing."*

# Conclusion

We live in a world where information and new ideas are transmitted instantly. Things are moving forward very quickly in the evolution of the human race. Today, more information is generated in a single day than was available in the entire lifetime of our grandparents.

In the past, it took decades for our culture to embrace new ideas and assimilate a new belief into our way of doing things. The idea that women are equal to men was at first laughed at, then ridiculed, then fought against violently, until finally it was integrated fully and society continued as if this had always been the case with an attitude that "of course it is so." This is the same course of development for any radical new concept before it becomes integrated into mainstream understanding.

This new idea I've presented, that our internal state is the premise for our external reality, is also in a process of integration. This idea was initially shunned, then adamantly fought and is now being embraced by millions. You will be somewhere along the continuum of this process as you too integrate this new understanding.

It is my intention that our society will release old fears and old ways of being, so that we embrace this deeper understanding of reality and fully integrate it into our systems of education and healthcare. This societal change begins with each of us individually. *Your impact is far greater than you can imagine.* Use these tools to assist you in coming to your own realization of this Truth.

Anything you desire to change in your world is within your capability of changing. The change begins within you. It does not come about by manipulating your situation or fighting against things you disagree with. The change comes when you embrace your frustration with the world as your own internal state. The only "problems" you have are inside you. The world is as it is. Your frustration or anger about it is what you can deal with and shift. Choose to shift this frustration within yourself. When you shift yourself, the world shifts. This is the way we create a reality where everyone wins.

The science of quantum physics shows us that there is nothing outside us that is not impacted by our observation of it.

If I feel sad for starving children in Africa, it is

to be cleared within me. If I feel angry about abused animals, that anger is my internal pollution. *When I take responsibility for my own negative states I become whole.* Thus, I am empowered to do what needs to be done to generate real change in the world. This empowerment changes the way my words are heard and the impact they have. This empowerment enables me to inspire others to behave in ways that are consistent with respecting our world and my needs. This empowerment creates a space of clarity wherein we all see Truth.

I invite you to apply these MindBody Tools and empower yourself so that you are awake and inspired and can assist in creating a beautiful world for yourself and for us all! Choose your favorites and share them with everyone. We all need a way out of delusion and into heaven on earth! It starts in your own body.

## DrKimD.com/Resources

# Acknowledgments

I'm very excited to be getting my work into the hands of others struggling to have ideal health and feel exhilarated about life. This message stems from my own personal journey of studying the body and its mechanisms from a very young age, and I'm so fortunate to have had the education I've had to help me develop this understanding. This is the first of multiple books that are already being written so I can give back from the wealth of wisdom I've received.

Thank you so dearly to The Universe for being on my side, always being there for me and bringing me through every challenge in my life to meet this moment! I am immensely grateful for having created this book and brought it to fruition.

Thank you to all of my mentors: Jane Carriero, D.O. and Donald Hankinson, D.O., for teaching me how to be a great osteopath; Greg Thompson, D.O., for all of your wisdom and getting me through residency without medication; Christiane Northrup, M.D. for your courage in paving the way and for telling me I could do it too.

Thank you to Joan Borysenko, M.D., Larry Dossey, M.D., and Herbert Benson, M.D., for your courageous and expansive work in the field of medicine. To Esther Hicks for your infinite wisdom and service. To Bruce Lipton for your outlandish willingness to tell the truth. Thank you to Nancy Risley for RYSE; discovering your work connected me to myself in a way that nothing else did. Thank you to Shiva Rea and Beryl Bender Birch for your immense yogini wisdom; working with you deeply inspired my every moment. Thank you to Regina Thomashauer for giving me so much permission to be absolutely everything that I am and to Debbie Rosas for helping me remember how to dance.

Thank you to all of my patients for sharing your deepest pains, and opening to receiving this work. Serving you has been an immense honor and something that has made me grow every day.

Thank you to Apollonia Fortuna for teaching me how to listen and be present. This, of all the things I have learned, is the skill that has most helped me to be of value to others.

Thank you to Paul Czeck for showing me your "B's," believing in me, and being one of the greatest friends I have ever had. Thank you to my "Providence College girls" for believing in me, being there for me, and always bringing me back to who I am. Thank you to Andrea Perella for being able to understand me no matter what I may say, and always making it matter.

Thank you to my godfather, Carmine, for shedding a tear every time I cross a finish line, and to all of my aunts and uncles, my niece, nephews and cousins. Thank you to my sister for being my cheerleader, and my brother for your support in coming to see me speak.

Thank you to my parents: my father for making me strong, and my mother for showing me what to do with it. You are the ones who deserve to celebrate my every success.

Thank you to my incredible husband, Mario. You mean more to me than anything in the world and you are my living proof every single day that my dreams are meant to come true. Marrying you and having our daughter are the things I am most proud of in my life. I may never fully understand the challenge I went through to get here, but it has awakened me to serve the world in a bigger way. Thank you for being on this journey with me.

# About the Author

Kimberly D'Eramo, D.O. is a board-certified Emergency Medicine physician trained in Osteopathic Manipulative Medicine, who has been studying MindBody Medicine for decades.

After completing her Bachelor's Degree in Chemistry and Biology at Providence College, she attended medical school at University of New England College of Osteopathic Medicine and did her residency training at Emory University in Atlanta. She went on to serve as faculty at two Colleges of Osteopathic Medicine.

Dr. Kim has been conducting live and online training programs in MindBody Medicine for the past several years, and has appeared multiple times on national television to awaken others to the power of the mind-body connection. She co-hosted the Top-10 podcast "The Thrive Doctors" with her husband, Dr. Mario Torres-Leon.

In addition to being a physician and author, she is also a professional speaker, educator and entrepreneur. She founded the American

Institute of MindBody Medicine to educate other physicians about applying MindBody Medicine in clinical practice to eliminate chronic illness.

Dr. D'Eramo currently resides in Durango, Colorado with her husband and their children.

*Subscribe at DrKimD.com to receive weekly video and audio resources in MindBody Medicine as well as information on her programs and resources.*

Photo courtesy of Allison Evans

# For more information on
# Dr. Kim D'Eramo
# please visit:

# DrKimD.com

## The Instant Elevation Program
This amazing program will show you that your AWARE-NESS is the key to your health, that your BREATH directly activates healing, and that raising your CONSCIOUSNESS translates to chemical, cellular, and brain changes that restore health!

Visit DrKimD.com/iep

## EFT Tapping Mini-Course
Dr. Kim's 5-video series will help you to induce powerful self-healing, increase your energy levels, and more! The Emotional Freedom Technique can be used anytime, any-where!

Visit DrKimD.com/eftcourse

## Audio Meditations
These audio meditations are designed to assist you in residing in Harmony so your body can heal!

To purchase please visit DrKimD.com/meditations

## Work Live with Dr. Kim
If you are interested in working with Dr. Kim, she regularly conducts live group programs as well as group and private retreats.

Visit DrKimD.com/health to join her next "Embracing Health" group.